Sephardic Jews

and the Spanish

Language

The Between Wanderings book series

These new translations of vintage books celebrate Jewish life from the 1850s to 1920s—a time of intense migration, changes and challenges for Jews around the world. Some of the books feature first-person accounts describing the era's Jewish communities, customs, folklore, synagogues, schools, foods and culture. The first titles in the series are:

1. *Sephardic Jews and the Spanish Language*
   by Ángel Pulido

2. *Jewish Immigrants in Early 1900s America: A Visitor's Account* — A photo booklet with text by Anatole Leroy-Beaulieu

For news of upcoming fiction and nonfiction releases, visit betweenwanderings.com.

Sephardic Jews and the Spanish Language

Ángel Pulido

Translated by
Steven Capsuto

Steven Capsuto
Books & Translation Services
New York

This book was first published in Madrid in 1904 in a mixture of Ladino and modern Spanish by Sucesores de Rivadeneyra under the title *Los israelitas españoles y el idioma castellano*.

Steven Capsuto:
P.O. Box 194, New York, NY 10113
steven@linguacaps.com

The Between Wanderings book series and blog:
betweenwanderings.com

Sephardic Jews and the Spanish Language/
Ángel Pulido (tr. Steven Capsuto). — Edition 1.3.
ISBN 978-0-9978254-0-4

Cover: Postcards circa 1910 depicting Jews in Salonika. The cards are derived from black-and-white photos taken in the late nineteenth or early twentieth century. Cover design: Steven Capsuto.

Book Layout ©2013 BookDesignTemplates.com

CONTENTS

ÁNGEL PULIDO FERNÁNDEZ

The author, circa 1880s.

Translator's preface

IN 1904, A SPANISH SENATOR wrote a book in praise of Sephardic Jews, the descendants of the Jews that Spain and Portugal had expelled in the 1490s at the height of the Inquisition. Senator Ángel Pulido's *Sephardic Jews and the Spanish Language* and its 1905 sequel, *Spaniards without a Country and the Sephardic Race*, were the centerpiece of his seventeen-year campaign to convince Spain's government and cultural institutions to reopen relations with the country's banished Jewish offspring. This book documents Sephardic life at a turning point: the period in the late nineteenth and early twentieth century when many young Sephardim were starting to reject the Spanish language that their ancestors had passed down through the generations for four centuries after the expulsion.

An avid Judeophile, Pulido was happy to step aside and let Jews speak for themselves. In fact, he devotes more than a third of this book to letters and photos sent to him by Sephardim in Turkey, Morocco, Austria, Romania and Palestine. In these letters, they describe their communities, families, schools, synagogues, culture and language, showing us their lives in the "Old Countries" more than a century ago. Most of the letters were written and published in Ladino, a form of Spanish also known as Judeo-Spanish or Judezmo, among other names. These personal narratives are so unusual and valuable that even today, Jewish scholars still quote, study and analyze Pulido's two books about Sephardic Jews. This translation marks the first time either volume has been available in English.

I first heard of Ángel Pulido Fernández in 2014, while doing background research for a genealogy article. For a month, I read everything I could find about Jewish communities in the Ottoman Empire in the early 1900s, and a pattern emerged quickly: most of the books—old and new—talked about a Spaniard called Dr. Pulido who, in his day, was called "the Apostle of the Sephardic Jews." Some writers offered little explanation, expecting readers to know who he was. Others quoted tantalizing excerpts from the Jewish correspondence in his books.

Who, I wondered, was this Dr. Pulido? A quick internet search suggested that he was an important figure. For instance, the web portal Sefardiweb.com devotes an entire section to "Corresponsales de Ángel Pulido" ("Ángel Pulido's Correspondents"); there is a statue of him in Madrid's main central park, the Retiro; and in 2005, the Jewish Federation of Spain presented its first annual Senator Pulido Award for service to the Jewish community.

After I finished writing my article, I sat down to read *Sephardic Jews and the Spanish Language* in the original Spanish and Ladino. The correspondence and photos fascinated me, as did the interpolated material from books, newspapers and magazines of the era. Occasionally, when the author went off on a tangent about Spanish politics or his country's post-colonial decline, my attention started to flag. But then suddenly I would find myself reading another revealing letter, or the charter and manifesto of a Sephardic student association, or a description of early Zionist settlements, or an article about Jewish education in the Middle East, or pages and pages of old Ladino proverbs and ballads. Besides excerpting existing material, the author also offers solid information about the Jews of Spain before and after Ferdinand and Isabella's infamous Alhambra Decree of 1492.

After the Expulsion

In March 1492, Spain gave its Jewish residents three heartbreaking options: 1) leave the country where they had thrived for eight centuries, 2) convert to Catholicism or 3) be killed. An estimated two hundred thousand chose exile, spreading across Europe, North Africa, Asia Minor, the Balkans and the Middle East. Many found safety in Muslim lands, especially in the Ottoman Empire. On hearing of the Spanish decree, the Ottoman sultan Bayezid II sent navy ships to rescue Jewish refugees and ordered his subjects to welcome them into the empire. Descendants of the Spanish exiles became known as Sephardic Jews, from the Hebrew *Sefardi*, meaning 'Spanish.' In 1496, Portugal banished its Jews as well (some of whom had fled there from Spain). Many of the Portuguese Jews followed the route of the Spanish exiles and merged into their communities, which is why the word *Sephardic* often describes Jews of Spanish and Portuguese ancestry alike.

For the next few centuries, Spain largely pretended the Jews had never been there, even as the country kept punishing alleged crypto-Jews (converts to Christianity, suspected of practicing Judaism in secret). From the 1500s to 1800s, it was illegal to practice any religion but Catholicism in Spain, and in all those years, few Spaniards ever knowingly met a Jew. In the country's dominant culture, the popular stereotype of this now-absent people was of immoral, greedy, god-murdering moneylenders whose banishment had made Spain a holier, more moral place. The paradox is that while Spain spurned the Jews, countless Sephardim revered their ancestral land. Many families spoke and wrote in Ladino, usually in the Hebrew alphabet, and gave their children and organizations Spanish names. Even in places where the language eventually died out, their liturgy and the names of many synagogues referred to places in Spain.

This one-sided love affair—with Spain playing hard to get and numerous Sephardim pining for their former country—continued into the 1860s. In 1868, after a revolution deposed Isabella II, Jewish leaders in other countries successfully petitioned the acting prime minister to rescind the 1492 decree. Jews could legally enter Spain again, though synagogues were still banned. The next year, a new Constitution established freedom of religion; in the 1880s, the Spanish Crown took the radical step of knighting a Moroccan Sephardic journalist; and in the 1880s and 1890s, Spain repeatedly offered asylum to Jews fleeing from the horrors of Russia's anti-Semitic pogroms and exclusionary laws. Then came Senator Pulido's campaign to reconcile Spain and the Sephardim, which he pursued from the 1900s to 1920s. Since then, Spain has twice offered a streamlined citizenship process for foreign Sephardic Jews: once from 1924 to 1930 and again from 2015 to 2018. In between, in the mid-twentieth century, the country also welcomed Jewish refugees from the Holocaust. By then, Jews were no longer a complete mystery to Spaniards.

The Genesis of This Book

In the summer of 1903, on a steamship from Serbia to Bulgaria, two men struck up an unlikely friendship. One was a Bulgarian-born rabbi, scholar, folklorist and school principal who lived in Romania: Rabbi Haim Moshe Bejarano, who would later become the chief rabbi of Turkey. He and his wife, Reyna, were traveling to distract themselves after the recent death of one of their daughters. The other man was a Catholic physician, member of the Spanish Parliament, newspaper contributor, and forensic anthropologist: Senator Ángel Pulido, one of the architects of Spanish health policy in his era. Pulido, his wife Emilia and their son and daughter were fleeing from a Macedonian uprising that had erupted during their vacation in the Balkans. The Spanish family had recently been discussing Sephardic Jews, as the senator's son had Sephardic friends in Vienna. Earlier that year, the son had written an article in the medical journal *El Siglo Médico*, calling for a pro-

Sephardic campaign much like the one his father would soon undertake.

The Jewish couple and the Spanish family chatted for ten hours on the ship. The rabbi's distraught wife spoke less than her husband, who sporadically paused to comfort her. His grief, though overwhelming, had not eclipsed his perennial desire to meet interesting people, especially Spaniards. Though the rabbi had never seen Spain, he venerated all things Spanish. The shipboard conversation ranged from Jewish history to world literature, from medicine to education, from travel to medieval ballads, and from current events to the evolution of Ladino. The rabbi's erudition and love of Spain surprised and moved the senator. Midway through the voyage, Ángel Pulido started to develop a plan: he would try to convince Spain's government, cultural institutions, intellectuals and businesses to reestablish relations with Sephardic Jews around the world, and to let Jews know they were welcome to settle in Spain if they wished.

Eleven weeks later, in November, he launched this campaign with a passionate speech in the senate. By the time he yielded the floor, he had convinced the minister of state to support an outreach to Ladino-speaking Sephardim. Jewish periodicals abroad reported on the speech, garnering the senator letters from Jews on several continents. Pulido soon began publishing some of these letters in the newspaper *El Liberal*, along with his articles about Sephardic culture and history. In 1904, in his early fifties, he wrote a six-article series for the popular weekly magazine *La Ilustración Espa-*

ñola y Americana, which he later expanded into what would become *Sephardic Jews and the Spanish Language.* He would continue to promote reconciliation between Spain and the Sephardic Jews into his late sixties, and would write on the subject into his seventies.

His first inspirations for the campaign were personal: he had found great pleasure over the years in conversations with Sephardim abroad, and he was fascinated with Jewish faith and culture. However, he was also motivated by potential economic benefits to his "unhappy country." Spain was in a sorry state in 1903. One system of government after another had collapsed, creating economic chaos and deep political rifts. Formerly a powerful empire, the country was reeling financially and psychologically from the loss of its colonies in the Americas, and seemed to have developed a national inferiority complex. The solution, Pulido suggested, was to "acquire" some of the half-million Spanish-speaking Jews abroad who, he speculated, adored Spain as much as Rabbi Bejarano did.

Pulido expected that some Sephardim would move to Spain while others would stay where they were. This, he reasoned, would bolster Spain's international trade with Turkey, Greece, Bulgaria, Romania and other countries with large Sephardic populations. Since Jewish merchants in those lands knew both Spanish and the local languages, he said, it would be easy to do business with them. His emphasis on practical benefits was evident in this book's original dedication page, printed in an elegant typeface suggesting a personal note from the author:

AL MINISTRO DE ESTADO.
Á LA ACADEMIA DE LA LENGUA.
Á LAS CÁMARAS DE COMERCIO.
Y Á LA ASOCIACIÓN DE ESCRITORES Y
ARTISTAS.

Esbozado en las siguientes páginas un problema de interés nacional, ojalá su exposición sirva para que las mencionadas Instituciones acometan la obra patriótica de aquistar un pueblo español diseminado por el mundo, y favorecer con ello al engrandecimiento de nuestros intereses lingüísticos, literarios y mercantiles.

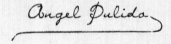

Dedication page of the Spanish edition.

TO THE MINISTER OF STATE.
TO THE ACADEMY OF THE LANGUAGE.
TO THE CHAMBERS OF COMMERCE.
AND TO THE ASSOCIATION OF
WRITERS AND ARTISTS.

These pages outline a matter of national interest, and I only hope this presentation will convince those Institutions to pursue the patriotic task of acquiring a Spanish people scattered across the globe, and thus help expand our linguistic, literary and commercial interests.

Angel Pulido

Pulido also argued that a cultural exchange, in which Spaniards and Jews could read each other's literature and journalism, would benefit both groups culturally and economically.

Some politicians and cultural figures supported the plan, but there were, of course, detractors. The more sympathetic critics accused him of being more sentimental than pragmatic when it came to Jews. They predicted that any economic benefits would be small and would occur too far in the future for the plan to be worthwhile. His less benevolent opponents included people such as Professor Joaquín Girón of the University of Salamanca. When Pulido invited him to meet for lunch to discuss the sequel volume, Girón refused to see him and instead put out his own 180-page book devoted to excoriating Pulido for—as he saw it—encouraging money-grubbing "Christ killers" to contaminate Spain with their "false Religion." Some other traditionalists also lambasted Pulido for advocating the "evil" principle of separation of church and state.

Pulido's project was a success all the same. Previously, Spanish periodicals had tended to mention Jews only in the past tense, as a long-ago people that had flourished alongside the ancient Egyptians and Greeks. Early in Pulido's campaign, the press began discussing modern-day Jews, and sometimes quoted letters from his books. His efforts also inspired other books on the topic and revived Spain's dormant Philo-Sephardic movement, in which well-known writers began donating volumes of Spanish literature to

Sephardic organizations abroad and initiated correspondence with prominent Jews.

In 1904, Pulido personally convinced the Royal Academy to start naming Sephardic intellectuals as corresponding members, starting with Rabbi Bejarano. The next year, amid publicity about Pulido's sequel book, Spanish newspapers reported on plans for a Jewish immigration society based in Madrid, designed to let Jews know it was now safe and legal to immigrate. The country's first two legally authorized synagogues in centuries appeared in 1909, and 1910 saw the founding of the Alianza Hispano-Hebrea (Hispano-Hebrew Alliance) to foster friendly ties between Spain and Sephardim. In 1920, Pulido helped to establish the Casa Universal de los Sefardíes (Universal Sephardic House), a Jewish cultural center in Madrid.

After a military coup in 1923, the new dictator Miguel Primo de Rivera disbanded the senate, but Pulido continued to advocate for public health reforms and for outreach to Sephardim. It is unclear how involved Pulido was in the new regime's 1924 decree offering citizenship to foreigners of Spanish ancestry, including Sephardim. That law established a 1931 deadline for applications, but Primo and his dictatorship expired the year before the offer did. In all, only about four thousand Jews applied, most of them from Salonika. Though the decree's impact was small, it set a precedent by recognizing a historical and moral link between Spain and the Sephardim. It was a forerunner of later Spanish laws that streamlined the citizenship process for Sephardic Jews, including the offer that is in effect at this writing.

The Book's Structure

Chapter 1 consists of six illustrated articles that originally appeared in the magazine *La Ilustración Española y Americana*, in the issues of February 8 to March 15, 1904. They account for 40% of the book and deal mainly with Sephardic Jews. Some (notably the second article) also include long detours into Spanish politics and the author's desire to expand Spain's international influence.

These untitled articles cover the following topics:

I—Introduction. In his travels, Pulido meets Jews who think of themselves as exiled Spaniards and who speak an archaic-sounding form of Spanish. He visits a Sephardic elementary school in Bucharest.

II—Europe's great nations are competing for linguistic dominance. Estimated numbers of Spanish-speaking Jews in different lands and their potential role in preserving Spanish. The history of Sephardic Jews and their relationship to Spain. A letter from Rabbi Bejarano about the early years after the expulsion.

III—Jewish periodicals abroad report on the author's recent senate speech, in which he urged Spain to reopen relations with Sephardim. Pulido receives correspondence from Sephardic Jews. Quotations from letters written by M. Gani, Lazar Ascher, Daoud Rousso and Rabbi Bejarano. The charter and manifesto of La Esperanza, an association of Sephardic students in Vienna.

IV—Sephardic identity is changing amid generational shifts and because of Jewish educational reforms, which put more emphasis on the French language. Younger Sephardim are drifting away from Ladino, since they do not consider Spanish a commercially useful language. The text of Sephardic ballads, proverbs and sayings.

V—Anti-Semitism. Ways to build relations with Sephardim. The Jews' status in the world amid changes and modernization. Sephardim are an admirable race. Famous Jews who contributed to humanity. A comparison of traditional Talmud-Torah schools and the modern schools run by the Alliance Israélite Universelle. Jews now hold prominent positions in the Ottoman Empire. Sephardic newspapers.

VI—Proposals for building strong ties between Spain and the exiled Spanish Jews. Freedom of religion in modern Spain. Eminent Sephardic Jews who might deserve honors from Spanish cultural organizations or the king. Conclusion.

The remaining chapters contain:

2. The author's letter to an organization of Sephardic university students in Vienna

3. Letters and photos from eight Sephardic Jews and two prominent Christian allies

4. A transcript of Pulido's senate speech and a discussion of responses to it

5. Spain's offers of asylum to Jewish refugees in the 1880s and 1890s

6. A French magazine article about the modernization of Jewish education in the Middle East, particularly in Alliance Israélite schools that attract Sephardic students

7. The 1902 budget of the Alliance Israélite Universelle

8. Part of a Spanish government report about Sephardic Jews in different regions of the Ottoman Empire

9. A letter to the author from the Viennese Sephardic student group, La Esperanza.

Cultural Context

All books are products of the era and culture that produced them, and *Sephardic Jews and the Spanish Language* reflects many biases and prejudices common to Spanish and Sephardic communities of the early 1900s, especially regarding gender. Pulido and his correspondents lived in societies that largely circumscribed women to the private sphere of the home. As a result, this book presents no female voices at all. The writers mention women only occasionally and seldom by name. Typically, they refer to women simply as this man's wife or that man's daughter. Moreover, Pulido's core argument could be paraphrased crudely as follows: Sephardic men are cultured, wise, productive and accomplished, and Sephardic women are physically attractive. On this last point, he asks us not to just take his word: he also quotes a former U.S. diplomat regarding Sephardic women's exotic allure, and quotes his own son who, on returning from a Sephardic dance, commented, "I didn't see even one ugly girl there." Even when reporting the death of Rabbi Bejarano's daughter, the author reduces her to her appearance: "She had died of tuberculosis at an age when her feminine charms (for she had been a splendid blonde beauty, we were later told in Bucharest) had reached their greatest expression."

The text does praise the era's Jewish school reforms, which aimed to give girls and boys the same education, but overall the book marginalizes women to a striking degree.

This even extends to the illustrations. Of the sixteen images in the original Spanish edition, only one depicts women: a photo of the Jewish girls' school in Damascus, which shows them from such a distance that their faces are indistinguishable. After the book came out, someone must have alerted Pulido to this problem, because his 1905 follow-up volume reflects a clear (if imperfect) attempt at gender inclusion. This English edition borrows some relevant photos from that sequel. For details, see "Image Sources" at the back of this volume.

The book also contains sporadic statements or insinuations that colonialism is good, that Ashkenazic Jews are inferior to Sephardim, that Ladino is not a real language, that humanity can be divided into "the civilized world and the East," and so on. This mix of great information and severe bias is most potent in the long magazine article that Pulido includes as an appendix. The French journalist Quercus gives us a rare, vivid look inside Jewish schools in Palestine and Syria, including the Jews' first modern vocational school and first agricultural college in what is now Israel. At the same time, however, his essay exudes disdain for all things non-French and non-European, scorn for the ancient Hebrews, and snide hatred toward observant twentieth-century Jews and Muslims.

Some modern readers will surely find this jarring, but even these biases give us valuable information about the subject matter: their existence tells us much about the world in which the book's writers and subjects lived.

About the Translation

Translating a 112-year-old book is a balancing act: each page demands trade-offs between being true to the language of the era and creating a text that modern audiences will find readable and comprehensible. The outdated terms I chose to use in this English edition include early-1900s place names such as Servia (now Serbia), Roumania (now Romania), Salonika (Thessaloniki) and Constantinople (Istanbul). A table of old and new place names appears just after this preface. In the English translation, as in the original, *the East* does not mean East Asia but rather Eastern Europe and the Middle East. The text sometimes mentions people writing in *rabbinical characters*. This can mean Rashi script (a set of semi-cursive Hebrew typefaces) or Solitreo (a related Sephardic handwriting style). Other dated terms in this translation include *Moslem* (because *Muslim* was not mainstream English until the 1940s) and sometimes *Hebrews* instead of *Jews*. The term *temple* (*templo* in the original) is used here as a generic synonym for *synagogue*, even though in today's English, temple refers almost exclusively to non-Orthodox synagogues. For clarity's sake, I avoided English words whose meaning has changed radically since 1904. For instance, in Pulido's era, Spanish *publicistas* and English *publicists* were authors who wrote about social issues, politics and current events. This translation calls them *journalists* if they wrote for periodicals. Similar concerns apply to *israelita*, which this edition typically translates as *Jew* or *Jewish* rather than *Israelite*.

One major dilemma was what to do with people's names. Personal names were very fluid at the time, and it was common to translate them from one language to another. In the original book, Pulido uses Hispanicized versions of names. For example, the men who were generally known as Haim Bejarano, Lazar Ascher and Daoud Rousso are referred to here as Enrique Bejarano, Lázaro Ascher and David Rousso (though at one point, the author slips and calls him Daoud). Some of them may have used Spanish names when speaking or writing in Ladino, but there is no easy way to find out who did and who did not. Therefore, I have retained Spanish names in the body of the book, but have used people's better-known first names in the notes and the subject index. For famous historical figures such as Maimonides, Judah Halevy and Queen Isabella, the translation uses the names by which they have traditionally been known in English.

Overall, I followed the original text closely. Besides stylistic adjustments (tailoring punctuation and sentence length to English custom) and the addition of footnotes, the only significant changes involved adding a title to Chapter 1 ("The magazine articles"), two paragraph breaks (in places where they add clarity) and a bibliography and index.

Pulido included some Spanish translations of foreign material in his book. When the source language was English, I tracked down the text and used the original wording. Where he translated from French, I worked from the French instead of retranslating his translation. The main exception is the letters from Daoud Rousso and Elias Pasha

Cohen, for which I did not have access to the original French manuscripts.

In translating poems and ballads (which appear here in English alongside the Ladino text), I usually focused on their meaning, without trying to recreate rhyme or meter. Except as noted, all footnotes are the translator's.

It took two years to research, translate, correct and annotate this volume, and it has been a labor of cultural and linguistic love. It is a privilege to help these voices speak in another language, and the timing could not be better. Just as I began drafting this preface in June 2015, I learned that the Spanish Parliament had finally approved a right of return for Sephardim without the previously imposed residency requirement. The offer has many restrictions—it is open only until 2018 and is not as comprehensive as the straightforward law that Portugal passed the same year—but it is still remarkable.

Some people have asked if I plan to translate Pulido's second book about Sephardim. That hefty volume, whose title we could translate as *Spaniards without a Country and the Sephardic Race*, is more problematic. Of its nearly seven hundred pages, fewer than half contain first-person accounts by Jews, and the letters are of a much less personal nature than those in this first book. The bulk of the sequel will only interest scholars of early-1900s Spain. So for now, my plan is to publish this first volume and then translate excerpts of *Spaniards without a Country* for my "Between Wanderings" blog (betweenwanderings.com). Eventually, I might consider an abridged English edition of the sequel. I am also working on translations of other books of Jewish interest from the 1850s to 1920s, mostly by Jewish authors. For information on upcoming titles, visit the blog.

For now, though, let's explore a world that no one alive today recalls: the world of Sephardim before the Holocaust, before World War I and before the Balkan Wars, in the years when Ladino-speaking Salonika was "the Jerusalem of the Balkans," when hundreds of Jews held high-ranking government posts in a vast Muslim empire, and when a politician in Madrid saw Jews as potential saviors of the Spanish language.

Steven Capsuto
New York
July 2016

A KEY TO 1904 PLACE NAMES

1900s name	2010s name
Adrianople	Edirne
Constantinople	Istanbul
Cordova	Cordoba
Galata	Karakoy
Haskeuy	Haskoy
Kalarash	Calarasi
Louvain	Leuven
Mazagan[1]	El Jadida
Mogador	Essaouira
Pera	Beyoglu
Persia	Iran
Philippopolis	Plovdiv
Plevna	Pleven
Rodosto	Tekirdag
Roumania	Romania
Rustchuk	Rousse
Salonika	Thessaloniki
Scutari	Uskudar
Servia	Serbia
Smyrna	Izmir
Stamboul (informal name)	Istanbul
Tetuan	Tetouan
Vilna	Vilnius
Yekaterinoslav	Dnipropetrovsk

---

[1] Mazagan became El Jadida in the nineteenth century. When this book was written, many people still used the old name.

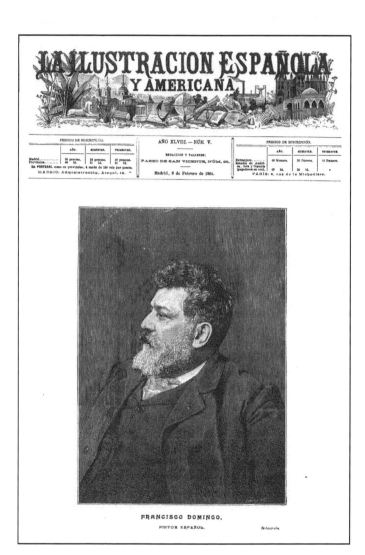

LA ILUSTRACION ESPAÑOLA Y AMERICANA

AÑO XLVIII. — NÚM. V.

REDACCIÓN Y TALLERES:

PASEO DE SAN VICENTE, NÚM. 20.

Madrid, 8 de Febrero de 1904.

FRANCISCO DOMINGO,

PINTOR ESPAÑOL.

The first part of this book originally appeared as a series of six articles in the weekly pictorial magazine *La Ilustración Española y Americana*, starting in the issue of February 8, 1904.

[1]

The magazine articles

I

A SPANIARD TRAVELING almost anywhere in Europe, especially in the East or the South, typically will have this pleasant surprise:

On his train or his ship, or at shops in countries and cities with native languages radically different from his own, he will notice strangers eavesdropping on his Spanish with astonishing frequency. They will listen intently and then strike up engagingly spontaneous conversations with him in a very peculiar Spanish, of highly erratic intelligibility. They will take conspicuous joy in introducing themselves as his countrymen from the East, and will gaily, warmly draw him into long dialogues about race, history and nationality. These are members of the far-flung race of Spanish Jews, whose existence and nature we in Spain view clumsily, with the greatest indifference, and with our usual shortsightedness and shallowness, whether we are government officials, scholars, historians, merchants or journalists.

It is no great novelty to say that Spanish Jews live in many European countries: almost everyone, and certainly any educated person, has heard this often and may even have heard comments about them. What would be new, though, would be to deign to examine the topic and assess its importance and meaning today, and look at its relationship to the multilingual education that powerful nations such as Germany, England, France and Italy sponsor at home and abroad as they compete with other lands for dominance. Surely, Spain could find ways to do what those countries must have done: take the aftermath of a dramatic event in our past—one that still has intense, powerful repercussions in much of Europe, Asia, Africa and even the Americas—and make it a public asset, a tool of Spain's international reach and a symbol of her influence.

This is highly important. I shall resist the urge to share all my copious information on the subject (which could appear elsewhere, perhaps in a book), and instead these articles will be an overview. Unless I am very clumsy about it, though, my gentle readers will notice quickly that germinating in this matter are weighty questions of culture, linguistics, commerce and international relations. Statesmen, scholars, journalists and merchants should face these issues and act on them promptly for the profit and glory of our unhappy country. Personally, when I appealed to the Minister of State (the Count of San Bernardo) on this topic in the Senate on the afternoon of November 13, and now, as I write about it in the cultured, enlightened Spanish magazine *La Ilustración Española y Americana*, the subject did not and does not strike me as theoretical, literary, linguistic or anecdotal. No, this is a question of great practical import and national benefit. So I intend to take it beyond the confines of a fairly curious pet topic and pursue a truly patriotic task—I dare not call it transcendental, though it should be—whose potential for action and development lies mainly with other institutions.

On August 31, 1883, I was on one of those lovely steamships that glide down the Danube from Vienna to Budapest. I was talking with my family on deck when three male passengers approached us. One—a thickset old man with a tidy gray beard, holding his hat in one hand—greeted me in perfect Spanish and said, "Excuse me, are you Spanish?"

"I am, indeed," I replied. "And so, I take it, are you."

"Yes, I am," he said. "But not Spanish from Spain. I am a Spaniard from the East."

I was surprised and frankly baffled at this enigmatic explanation. Another aged member of the trio, who had kept a respectful distance until then, decided to join the conversation. He surprised me further by saying, "I'm a Spaniard, too, but from Servia."

"I'm sorry," I said, not understanding a type of statement I would hear so often in the future, "but I don't see what you mean about your nationality."

"We are Spanish Jews," the first added, smiling.

"Ah, there we have it!" I exclaimed, using a particularly Spanish turn of phrase.

Another Spanish Jew introduced himself, and the four of them joined my family's party of three. All seven of us then had a long, animated discussion, asking tirelessly about a thousand aspects of each other's lives and customs. The whole time, our companions showed a strange sense of Spanish identity and an inexplicable pride and gratitude at our having met. Clearly they wanted to assist and please us, which was of great help in the Hungarian capital, where we all left the ship together. I jotted down their names and mentioned them at the time in letters published in the newspaper *El Liberal,* later collected in one of my books, *Plumazos de un viajero*: Semaria Mitrany was a native of Kalarash, Roumania, and the other three—Moisés Isak and his son and Arón-Leví—were from Belgrade, Servia.

Two decades later, last year, as the sun rose on August 24, 1903, my family and I left Belgrade at 5 a.m. on a steamship bound for Orsova. We were fleeing from Macedonian insurgents and hoping for safe passage to Constantinople via the Black Sea. On deck just out of port, we realized our conversation had piqued the curiosity of a short, gaunt, venerable-looking man, accompanied by a visibly grief-stricken, silent, gray-haired woman, also compactly built, on whom he lavished phrases of consolation in that strange Spanish we had heard before.

We all soon fell into conversation and, after mutual introductions, we learned he was a noted scholar from Eastern Europe, a renowned polyglot conversant in many European and Asian languages: Arabic, Hebrew, German, English, French, Italian, Spanish, Greek, Armenian, Slavic[1] and Roumanian, among others. He was the headmaster of the Spanish-Jewish School in Bucharest, traveling with his wife to assuage their grief over the recent loss of a beautiful daughter. She had died of tuberculosis at an age when her feminine charms (for she had been a splendid blonde beauty, we were later told in Bucharest) had reached their greatest expression.

He was of a different social class than the Jews mentioned above—he is a learned rabbi, while they described themselves as wealthy merchants—but he, too, exuded a strange elation and pride at our meeting, a certain lively sense of brotherhood, which he expressed in exclamations and phrases so hyperbolic and flattering that they sometimes bewildered us. At one point, for instance, I recall him returning to his disconsolate wife, who stood motionless staring out at the river. "Do you see how Providence cares for us and consoles us?" he said to her. "Today He is giving us the pleasure of traveling on this ship and meeting these people, who are from Spain, from our beloved mother country, and of becoming their friends. Do you see how good God is?" And so with soft

---

[1] At the time, some people informally referred to Bulgarian, Serbian and other non-Russian Slavic languages as if they were dialects of a single language called *Slavic*.

words and exquisite tenderness and grace, he celebrated our happy meeting and the chance to talk with native Spaniards, *his brothers*, and to hear news, information and expressions of culture, tolerance and love for things authentically Spanish, of which he said he so often dreamed.

I was intrigued, even moved by this pure, legendary love for his remote ancestors' homeland, this heartfelt tribute of connection and affection for children of Spain whom they had only just met casually for the first time. At that moment, I knew I wanted to build a friendship with this impressive man whom fate had put in my path. I wished to gain some personal knowledge through his diligent indulgence, and mount a campaign to open relations that I consider appropriate.

From 6 a.m., when we first exchanged words, until 4 p.m., when we disembarked in Orsova and the Jewish couple transferred to their ship bound for Bulgaria, we never stopped talking. In that time, I came to appreciate his deep knowledge of old Spanish prose writers and ballads, his literary Atticism, his mastery of the expressive arts and many languages, his gift for storytelling, his familiarity with countless long-ago tales and fables from Spanish literature, and other varied evidence that here was a superior, truly erudite man. Later, through comments from people in Constantinople and Bucharest, I learned that this fine gentleman, Mr. Enrique Bejarano (for that is his name), was a scholar with an established, exemplary reputation through-

ENRIQUE BEJARANO
HEADMASTER OF THE SPANISH-JEWISH
PRIMARY SCHOOL FOR BOYS IN BUCHAREST

out the East.[2]

---

[2] The author's new friend was Rabbi Haim Moshe Bejarano (1850–1931), who later became the chief rabbi of Adrianople (1910–19) and of Turkey (1920–31). He was a scholar, congregational rabbi, folklorist, translator and school administrator.

Born in the Ottoman city of Eski Zagra (now Stara Zagora, Bulgaria), Bejarano showed an early talent for languages and religious studies. As a teenager, he devoured Jewish texts at a yeshiva while also studying the Koran in Arabic with a Muslim neighbor. He was wed at eighteen to a thirteen-year-old girl he had never met named Reyna. They would go on to have a large family. In his twenties, he worked as a schoolteacher and rabbi in Bulgaria, until the region became a battleground in the Russo-Turkish War. After a bombing killed his mother and one of his children in 1877, he moved the family to Romania, where he would stay for decades.

In Bucharest, he worked as a cantor and rabbi at the Great Spanish Temple; as headmaster of a prestigious primary school for boys, the Şcoala Primară de Băieţi Israelită-Spaniolă; and as a university professor. His writings include a collection of old Spanish proverbs that were still popular among the Sephardim centuries after the expulsion. Rabbi Bejarano maintained scholarly correspondence with leading Jewish and non-Jewish writers, theologians and philosophers. His correspondents included Miguel de Unamuno, as well as the author and translator Elisabeth of Wied, who by then was the queen consort of Romania. She eventually knighted him.

At Senator Pulido's urging, the Spanish Royal Academy made Rabbi Bejarano its first Sephardic corresponding member in 1904. The Sephardic congregations of Adrianople unanimously elected him as their chief rabbi in 1909, and Sultan Mehmed V confirmed the appointment. Three years later, this sultan decorated him with the Order of the Medjidie for his service to the Ottoman Empire. Rabbi Bejarano lived the final decade of his life in Constantinople, where he was the much-loved chief rabbi of Turkey.

Historical sources give his name in many forms. First name: Chaim, Chayim, Enrike, Enrique, Haim, Hayim or Haym. Last name: Becerano, Bedjerano, Bejarano, Bejerano or Bidjarano.

On hearing of my journey and profession, he promptly provided me with two letters written in Spanish, in rabbinical characters, addressed to Drs. Elías and Isaac Pasha, physicians to the Sultan of Turkey.[3] Surely he would have given me others related to famous figures in most of the eastern nations had I needed and requested them, as he took extraordinary pleasure in pleasing me.

A few days later in Bucharest, my wife, my children and I had the pleasure of visiting the Spanish-Jewish school where this teacher's family lived. I also met his charming daughters, whose keen intelligence and knowledge made sense when we learned that they, like their good father, were educators. We examined the classrooms of the new school building, which had cost 130,000 francs to build, raised by subscription among the Spanish Jews, and we could appreciate its elegant architecture and layout. It resembles a hotel, and its classrooms, reserved for children of

---

[3] Dr. Elias Cohen (1844–unknown) and Dr. Isaac Molho (1830s/40s–1919): senior medical officials of the Ottoman Empire, generally known as Elias Pasha and Isaac Pasha.

In 1884, Dr. Cohen became the first Turkish Jew elevated to the rank of pasha, the highest title of male nobility in the empire. By the time this book appeared, he was the sultan's personal physician. He was also active in protecting the safety and interests of Jews in that part of the world.

Dr. Molho, honored with the title of pasha in the 1880s, was the longtime chief health inspector of the Ottoman Imperial Navy. When this book appeared, he was president of the Jewish Community Council of Constantinople, on whose board he had served on many occasions.

Some sources give Dr. Cohen's name as Eliyas Kohen. Dr. Molho's first name sometimes appears as İzak.

one sex or the other, are little but well ventilated, as if meant for small classes. They contain few teaching materials.

Founded in 1730, the school has a four-year elementary education program. It teaches secular subjects in Roumanian, the country's language, but the Catechism, Bible and Religion are taught in Spanish.

As previously mentioned, headmaster Bejarano is also a rabbi: his synagogue, built in a handsome Byzantine style, stands next to the school.[4] He was born in December 1850 in the small city of Stara Zagora, where he studied theology. At eighteen, he became a religion teacher and at twenty-two, he began learning modern languages, an interest he has embraced ever since "with great devotion and happiness" (his words).

His strong love for all things Spanish seems especially remarkable since he has never seen Spain. He has children studying in Paris and has visited that city, but has never come to a land that he evokes with powerful emotion and which he dreams of visiting, as if that were some happy, almost ineffable possibility.

At the school's awards ceremony, held on June 25, children generally recite compositions in various languages as proof of their learning. At the 1903 celebration last year, a little boy recited this poem, written by Mr. Bejarano himself:

---

[4] Rabbi Bejarano preached at the Great Spanish Temple (also known as Kahal Kadosh Gadol and Kahal Grande). It stood at 10 Nedru Voda Street in Bucharest from the 1810s until its destruction in a pogrom in 1941. For photos of the synagogue and more information, see the letters from Rabbi Bally and Lazar Ascher starting on page 146.

THE SCHOOL
THE SPANISH-JEWISH PRIMARY SCHOOL FOR BOYS
(BUCHAREST)

LA LENGUA ESPAÑOLA

A ti, lengua santa,
á ti te adoro,
más que á toda plata,
más que á todo oro.
Tú sos la más linda
lenguaje;
á ti dan las ciencias
todo el ventaje.
Con ti nos hablamos
al Dios de la altura,
patrón del Universo
y de la Natura.
Si mi pueblo santo
él fué captivado,
con ti, mi querida,
él fué consolado.

THE SPANISH LANGUAGE

Thou, holy language,
Thee I adore,
More than all silver,
More than all gold.
Thou art the most beauteous
Language;
To thee all fields of knowledge
Give every advantage.
Through thee we talk
To God above,
Lord of the Universe
And of Nature.
Although my holy people
Has been captive,
Through thee, my beloved,
It was consoled.

An eyewitness to that school celebration reported that as the boy recited this heartfelt poetry, several in the audience wept. This exaltation of their mother tongue stirred deep religious feelings and a homesickness for the dear, lost land where their ancestors' ashes lie, a country whose tragically exiled offspring they still consider themselves.

We could easily impose negative interpretations on this. That would, however, seem childishly impetuous (unforgivable in one who has already traveled most of his life's road, sometimes pondering and often fighting in the heated battles that nations, races, communities and individuals pitch to protect their interests and serve their egos). Faced with historical sentiment that turns a language into the most familiar, beloved symbol of a people who have been banished and persecuted the world over, we might well see it as fodder for coarse speculation: "Isn't that just like a Jew, eh?!" No, that is not the point and we must not stoop to that crude level, because the scene offers worthier, more brotherly aspects that can and should benefit our country abundantly. Such brotherhood should be our focus, as it has been for some of our countrymen, though very few. For instance, the late Marquis of Hoyos and our current Chief Customs Officer, Mr. Juan B. Sitges, both devoted studies to the crucial topic of Spanish Jews.

In Vienna, where the late Marquis served as Spanish Ambassador, Dr. Beer told us this noble aristocrat once wrote a fascinating, unpublished report on the Spanish Jews of that city, the Austro-Hungarian capital, and that a copy survives in the National Library. Eager to read it, we asked permission from the widowed Marchioness. That distinguished lady informed us that several copies exist, including one at the Royal Academy of Moral and Political Sciences, where the author had meant to use it as his induction speech after being named to that body. His death prevented this. The Academy, she said, plans to publish this important work in its annals this year.

We learned of Mr. Sitges' research when we heard this great patrician speak of his longtime interest in the subject. He talked of the correspondence he had sought to establish with renowned Spanish Jews of the East, including Mr. Bejarano; of his failed attempts to convince the government, under several administrations, to open relations with Spanish Jews; of his dedication in urging prominent Jews and some Ministers of Public Works to prevent the potential destruction of El Tránsito synagogue in Toledo. That building's age-old history makes it a revered, important site, and Mr. Sitges wants it restored before it collapses and we lose one of the most exemplary gems of the imperial city. These and other projects attest to his passion for and grasp of this engaging, thought-provoking topic.

But what speaks for this cause better and louder than any earnest commitment from Spaniards is the commitment and dedication of the Jews themselves. In some of the many countries where Spanish Jews reside, they are now trying to institute measures and educational programs not just to prevent the extreme corruption or deformation of Spanish—a language they have passed down from parent to child—but to avoid its complete loss to encroachment by the languages of the great empires. They know that tongues such as German, English and French are battling to gain speakers and increase the number of people who use them for their needs, whether scientific, literary or commercial.

That, however, is a separate subject, to be addressed in our next article.

EL TRÁNSITO SYNAGOGUE
DETAIL OF THE FAMOUS SYNAGOGUE FOUNDED BY
SAMUEL LEVI IN TOLEDO, SPAIN

II

SHOULD A COUNTRY CARE whether people use and promote its language abroad? If so, is it obliged to expend money and effort to achieve this?

It is fair to say that such questions arise only in Spain and in nations that never look beyond their borders when pondering the great purposes of public life: they arise only in cultures that never bother to study their own national riches. Sadly, given Spain's incurable national flaws, her recent governments have had troubled, brief, conflict-ridden lives. In that context, the ordinary, positive pursuits that I am proposing sound delicate and fanciful. Other countries, however, manage them perfectly with satisfying results.

Think for a moment about the courses that are mainstays of education in the world's great nations (the most cultured nations, which thereby possess greatness of the highest order). Notice the care they take in two areas: ensuring that their schools, lycées, academies, etc. teach the world's most widely spoken languages, while also ensuring that their own language is taught and studied abroad. This makes the human word the most relevant, productive tool for their international relations, and for expanding the spirit and richness of their heritage. Nothing could be more natural!

The proof is so pervasive and compelling that we could call it a truism. And yet, since I refuse to make ad hoc assertions in a serious treatise, I shall stick to facts and observations from my recent travels in Europe: I shall recall, for instance, the Dante Alighieri Society's convention in Udine in late September, with its heated and interesting debates about plans to open an Italian university in Trieste. The Society president, Pasquale Villari, urged Italian youth to become apostles to spread their gorgeous national language around the world, and he encouraged the society to overcome the problems that its educational programs were facing in Tunisia and Marseilles. Amid frantic applause, I heard Poscia Zaniboni of its Naples chapter announce the establishment of Italian libraries on ships carrying emigrants. I shall also recall that the short courses at Swiss universities during academic holidays included multiple classes designed to improve language skills, mainly in German and French. I shall recall how France budgeted public funds for special universities and schools in other countries, including the French University at Athens and the French Medical School in Beirut.[5] In the East, France hoped to retain the intellectual sway she had long held in so many countries, now eroded by international competition and increasingly hostile attitudes in some nations. In Germany and Austria, for example, there has been a strong reaction against the use of foreign languages. In that context, they have instituted free classes for students and teachers from other lands, to further nationalize education and spread the German language more effectively. I shall recall Hungary's

---

[5] A reference to the École Française d'Athènes, which the French government helped to establish in Greece in 1846, and the École Française de Médecine in Beirut, founded by Jesuit priests in 1883.

stern, menacing laws that imposed the use of its Magyar language, thus paralyzing parliamentary life and government operations, and creating an increasingly grave, terrible threat to the peace and hegemony of its Germanic partner, Austria. I shall recall Roumania—that new, burgeoning state—whose illustrious, patriotic Ministers of Public Education, including Ionescu, Poni and Marzescu, deserve credit for effective, highly advanced education laws. Roumania has been nurturing its national soul, and its Roumanian language has overtaken the others, chiefly French, that once predominated there. I shall recall how even Turkey—relaxing its old fierce, staunch fanaticism and opening itself to intellectual nourishment and an exchange of ideas with the most advanced nations—took a large step by establishing its grand new military and civilian School of Medicine. Built in Scutari, the school was inaugurated last year by the Sultan himself on November 30, 1903. Turkey endowed it with all the resources and the broad variety of studies that modern scientific education demands. The only thing physically separating Stamboul's old medical schools from the new one is the churning currents of the divine Bosphorus. However, the essence and spirit of the courses show that the old and new schools are separated by the immensity of a splendid civilization. The new school's medical curriculum—which the Sultan approved in his decree of November 12, 1903—includes a full eight consecutive years of French and German, from the first year of secondary school until the third year of university, to ensure its students' place in the serious study of a field taught entirely in German. I shall recall... But why go on? Why invoke endless exotic colleges, teachings, publications, institutes and so on? They catch the attention of any traveler who notices what nations now do to promote their interests amid international competition, and who therefore appreciates the value of languages. How can we ignore the ongoing contest among dominant races and powerful states such as England, Germany and France, as they aim to infuse other countries with their language, their very essence, through newspapers, school resources and other forms of expression in their language?

Contrast that with our unhappy Spain, a prodigiously fertile mother of other nations that were called to glittering destinies.[6] Spain, who imposed her speech through blood and sacrifice in the Americas and in the Magellanic and Antillean archipelagos, has much more than half a million Jewish families[7] scattered through nearly every European country and across Asia and Africa: her forgotten children who still defend the national language, in somewhat adulterated form, against the many circumstances that would extinguish it.

How many Spanish Jews are there? How interested are they in preserving the Castilian tongue? What are they doing to safeguard our language? Such relevant queries deserve comment.

---

[6] A reference to Spain's former colonies in the Americas.

[7] This is an inconsistency: most of the estimates that the author cites suggest half a million Sephardic Jews, not half a million Sephardic families.

⁓

I know of no statistics on the number of Spanish Jews worldwide, and I wonder if such figures exist. Given the dispersion of this race and the misfortunes it suffers everywhere (to varying degrees, depending on the country), I fear there may be no such numbers. Surely their population and geographic range are greater than what rumor or a quick glance suggests, and I, for one, can say I found them in every European country I have visited, which includes all but the northernmost lands.

The preface to Kayserling's interesting *Diccionario bibliográfico de autores judíos españoles y portugueses*, published in Strasbourg (1890), tells us the following:[8] After Queen Isabella of Spain and King Manuel of Portugal expelled the Jews from the Iberian Peninsula, the exiles took refuge in Italy, France, the various provinces of the Turkish Empire, the Netherlands, England, Hamburg and Vienna. Wherever they went, they brought their mother tongue. "They took from here our language," wrote Gonzalo de Illescas in the sixteenth century, "and still gladly preserve and use it; and it is true that in the cities of Salonika, Constantinople, Alexandria and Cairo, and in other trading cities and in Venice, they neither buy nor sell nor transact business in any language but Spanish. And

---

[8] Most of this paragraph is an abridged quotation from M. Kayserling, *Biblioteca española-portugueza-judaica: dictionnaire bibliographique des auteurs juifs, de leurs ouvrages espagnols et portugais et des oeuvres sur et contre les juifs et le judaïsme*, Strasbourg: Charles J. Trubner, 1890, x.

in Venice I met numerous Jews from Salonika who, young though they were, spoke Castilian as well as or better than I."

This clearly indicates that Spanish Jews ventured beyond Europe and fled to countries on neighboring continents.

In a letter on this subject, Mr. Juan B. Sitges tells me that our current ambassador to Portugal, Mr. Polo de Bernabé, made a cursory estimate of the number of Spanish Jews in the East when he was running the Commerce Division of the Ministry of State. He adds that the division's archives should still have a relevant report that Mr. Antonio de Zayas prepared in Constantinople, dated August 15, 1897, about the social, political and commercial status of Hebrews in three countries: the Ottoman Empire, the kingdom of Roumania and the principality of Bulgaria. Mr. Zayas estimated that fifty-two thousand Spanish-speaking Jews live in Constantinople, fifty thousand in Salonika, twenty-two thousand in Smyrna and lesser numbers in many other municipalities.

My illustrious friend Dr. A. N. Psaltoff of Smyrna wrote to me this month, on February 1, saying that Smyrna is home to twenty-five thousand Spanish-speaking Jews, Salonika sixty thousand, Constantinople forty thousand, and he understands that Spanish is also spoken by all the Jews of European Turkey and Asia Minor.

Mr. Enrique Bejarano, the scholarly headmaster of the Spanish-Jewish School in Bucharest, supplied the following information (and as you will see, his writing reflects some of the peculiarities of Judeo-Spanish):[9]

> The current number of Spanish Jews in the East could
> well be almost 471,900. They are scattered mainly
> through the Asian and European parts of Turkey, as well
> as Bulgaria, Servia, Roumania, Greece, and even small
> numbers in Austria, England and France, but primarily
> Turkey.

My son, young Dr. Pulido Martín, has been doing his residency in Vienna for a year, broadening and specializing his medical studies, and I have asked him to gather information from the large Hebreo-Spanish colony there (which we shall discuss in another article). He says that in Bosnia there are about ten thousand Jews, most of whom speak Spanish; in Servia about eight thousand, mostly in the capital, Belgrade; in Sofia, probably around ten thousand and in all of Bulgaria thirty thousand to thirty-five thousand.

In Roumania there are just four communities: in Bucharest, the largest; in Craiova, the second largest; and in Turnu Severin and Kalarash.

The biggest colony of all is in Salonika, where Spanish is so prevalent that traders learn the language before traveling there.

---

[9] An English translation cannot convey the differences between Ladino and modern Spanish. Readers who wish to see these letters in their original form can find the Spanish edition of the book online. At this writing, the clearest, most complete copy seems to be the PDF file at the Biblioteca Digital de Castilla y León: http://bibliotecadigital.jcyl.es/i18n/catalogo_imagenes/grupo.cmd?path=10067842&posicion=1.

Central and Northern Europe are also home to some, though Jews of Portuguese descent are perhaps more frequent there. In our travels through Holland and Belgium, we have seen Spanish Jews. In Amsterdam, Frankfurt, etc., we have walked through Jewish neighborhoods where some of the population was of Spanish origin. And certainly after reading Kayserling's long roster of Spanish and Portuguese Jewish authors in his aforementioned *Diccionario bibliográfico*, listing countless texts published in Spanish or Ladino (Judeo-Spanish) in the Netherlands, we realize the Dutch nation must still have many descendants of those Jews, who included many distinguished writers of nonfiction.

England can also be said to have some, based on the information mentioned earlier. That reminds me of Menasseh ben Israel,[10] born in Lisbon but very Spanish in his writings. This illustrious man was determined to reopen England to the Jews, who had been banned from there since the reign of Edward I. So he went to London in 1655 and negotiated personally with Cromwell, who treated him with esteem and granted him a pension. However, the Jewish sage died soon after, in 1657 in Middelburg, where he was buried with the following epitaph in Spanish:

---

[10] Menasseh ben Israel (1604–57): a Portuguese-born Dutch rabbi, kabbalist and publisher, renowned for his scholarship, oratory skills and—late in life—for his negotiations with Cromwell.

Menasseh's students included Benedict de Spinoza, and his social circle included notable writers, theologians, philosophers and artists, including Rembrandt. Some modern scholars suggest he may have been born after his parents fled Lisbon, not in the city itself, where the Inquisition suspected the family of being crypto-Jews.

No murió, porque en el cielo
Vive con suprema gloria,
Y su pluma y su memoria
Inmortal dexa en el suelo.

He did not die, for high in Heaven
He lives on in supreme glory,
While his memory and his pen
He leaves, immortal, here on Earth.

Russia, too, has Spanish Jews in many of her largest cities, including Odessa, a port on the Black Sea.

Asia Minor is brimming with them, and they also abound in Tripoli, Tunisia, Morocco and Egypt, in other words throughout North Africa.

The Spanish Jews' dispersion must therefore have been very great, largely because of the political environment in the countries on the Old Continent and the considerable power of Spain. We can see proof of this dispersion in the Spanish-language Bible printed in Ferrara in March 1553, translated from the Hebrew. Its publishers state, "In every province of Europe and elsewhere, the Spanish tongue is most copious and held in the highest esteem, and so I have striven to make this, our Bible in Spanish, the most faithful to the Hebrew..."

As a result, there must be countless Spanish-speaking Jews all over Europe, but there is reason to believe that the most thriving, populous colonies are in the East. All the reasonably trustworthy information we have read and heard lets us put the number as high as half a million. This is the figure Daoud Rousso posits in an important letter that will appear in a later article. We received the same estimate from vice-admiral Dr. Elías Pasha, physician to the Imperial Palace, in another letter addressed to us from the Queen of Cities.[11]

In brief, statistically, there must be more than half a million Jews who speak Spanish as their native language, residing in almost all European nations and many countries of Asia Minor and North Africa. They thus form a vast, important network of expatriated Spaniards with a relatively strong inclination to feel currents of sympathy for their legendary motherland.

This last assertion requires testimony and evidence.

Spanish Jews clearly profess a great love for Spanish, the language of their forefathers, which they use at home and in the intimate teaching of religion. It is also true that Spanish, a language ever more corrupt worldwide, is losing ground to the universal dominance and greater social utility of English, French and German. The Jews relegate Spanish to the sanctuary of the home; Spanish speakers everywhere neglect its structure and vocabulary; and Spanish governments have ignored it completely for more than

---

[11] *Queen of Cities:* a nickname for Constantinople.

four centuries, never bothering to notice or show interest in so delicate a problem as the national treasure that is our language. Naturally it has lost much of its charm and faces serious threats of extinction, a dreadful prospect.

Better, more detailed explanations than I could hope to produce can be found in excerpts from letters that I was honored to receive from distinguished Jews, whose sentiments and judgments will surely arouse the readers' interest. We shall respect their writing style and leave it intact.[12]

Let us begin with the learned Mr. Bejarano. These paragraphs, from an extensive letter to us dated November 20, 1903, are commendable for their heartfelt expression:

> With your pure soul and generous heart, you, like other friends in Spain, wish to pursue close relations with my brothers who were exiled unjustly from that sweet country, from that beneficent heaven, more than four centuries ago.
>
> For twenty years, I have maintained literary correspondence with certain scholarly gentlemen in Spain who wished to develop such relations: they hoped to undo the disgrace that their ancestors committed in expelling such a peaceful, docile, sweet, innocent people from their nests, all because of the ambitions of lawless, faithless men.

---

[12] In their everyday lives, most of Pulido's Jewish correspondents wrote Ladino in the Hebrew alphabet. When writing to him, however, they wrote it phonetically in Latin characters. Pulido's book generally preserves their distinctive spelling, word choice and style, to give his Spanish-speaking readers a sense of what Ladino sounds like.

[...]

God, who reads all secrets and knows the truth, can witness whether we might bear or hold a grudge or even ill will, but we still lament the sad result: a desolating exile and the painful memory of those illustrious sages who, from within Spain, shone like the sun and sent their rays of knowledge out through all the universe. They were Spain's glory and the glory of the Jewish people! All erased by one edict: Let there be darkness!!...[13]

Today we silently hear that mournful, sighing old saying:

> Yo sufro, Señor,
> Yo sufro tu saña;
> Perdí mi amor,
> Mí cara España!

---

[13] **PULIDO'S NOTE:** Who has not heard of the many wise, illustrious Jewish figures celebrated in Spain in different eras! The list would be too long to include here, but let us briefly cite: In Cordova, Hasdai ibn Shaprut in the court of Abd-al-Rahman III, who corresponded with the king of the Khazars (tenth century); Samuel Naghrela and his son Joseph, ministers in Granada; R. Yuda, under Alfonso VI, and the most famous of all, Samuel Levi, under Pedro the Cruel. In Portugal, King Ferdinand brought Dom David Negro and Dom Judah into his palace; Mr. Isaac Abravanel served as a minister for five consecutive years, under Alfonso V of Portugal and Ferdinand of Aragon; and other important men who, from the time of the Visigoths and Emirs and Caliphs until the exile, flourished in Spain with their profound learning and peerless talents, even rivaling those of their masters, and many of whom had tragic endings. Sages: Salomon Gaberul of Malaga (Avicebron), born in 1021; Ibn Yashush of Toledo, 1055; Halevy of Castile, 1086; Ibn Ezra, 1089; Ibn Daud of Cordova, 1180; Maimonides of Cordova, 1134, and Nachmanides of Geronda [Gerona], 1194.

> I bear Thy wrath,
> I bear the pain
> Of a love that's lost:
> My cherished Spain!

[...]

Most of these Jews speak Spanish more or less fluently. They still retain the character of the old native land: the air of the *hidalgo*, that inborn purity and calm; the penetrating gaze; the Spanish or Portuguese grace; in short, the customs they inherited from ancestors who cultivated them so carefully there. They possess, I might add, a solidarity and mutual affection among themselves.

Disinherited by fate, bound together by law and faith, united by pain, they arrived in hospitable countries, especially the Ottoman Empire, where His Majesty Sultan Bajazet issued an Imperial Order ensuring them a fine welcome.[14] They seem to have sworn a sacred friendship to help one another for better or for worse, in sickness and in health.

---

[14] Sultan Bayezid II (1447/48–1512, reigned 1481–1512). When Spain expelled its Jews in 1492, the sultan sent naval ships there to help evacuate the refugees. He offered them citizenship and proclaimed that, on pain of death, no one was to mistreat the Jews or impede their entry into the Ottoman Empire. It is true that non-Muslims did not have full legal equality in the empire, and there were certainly incidents of anti-Jewish violence and illegal forced conversions. Even so, at the time, this Islamic empire was a safer, more welcoming place for Jews than most of Christian Europe.

PULIDO'S NOTE: The Ottoman annals tell us that this monarch once told his courtiers, "You call Ferdinand a wise king—the very man who impoverished his own country to enrich mine!"

On arrival, they formed communities with the blessed aim of loving each other till death should them part.

Despite persecution, these good souls showed a unique ability to forget past wrongs and preserved the flame of their ardent love for the ancestral land from which they were ripped so cruelly. It pleased them to name their communities and even their new holy synagogues after places in Spain: the *Castilian* Jewish Community, the *Portuguese* Community, the *Aragonese* or *Cordovan* Community; the *Catalan* Synagogue, the *Mayor* Synagogue, the *Seville* or *Aragon* Synagogue, and so on.

To preserve the memory of their sweet Spain and not blot it from recollection, Jews took the names of their former cities as surnames: Alcalá, Alhueté, Alpojarre, Beja, Bejarano, Cordova, Cortez, D'avila, D'Erera, Gheron, León, Medina, Miranda, Navarro, Peñas, Segura, Soriano, Sevilla, Toledo, Todela, Taragano, etc.

Not satisfied with that, these victims of destiny, out of love for this language—which some say that God uses to speak to the angels in Heaven—started to name their children using certain Spanish adjectives, names of plants, birds, precious stones, etc.

Male names: Angel, Amado, Blanco, Benveniste, Bueno, Conorte, Comprado, Climente, Caro, Doño, Donoso, Galano, Querido, Presente, Santo.

Female names: Angela, Alta, Amada, Alegría, Alhavaca, Buena, Bella, Bienvenida, Blanca, Bruneta, Cara, Clara, Consuela, Diamante, Dona, Delicada, Dolza, Estrella, Esmeralda, Esperanza, Estimada, Flor, Fermosa, Galana, Gracia, Gentila, Hermosa, Joya, Luna, Linda, Morena,

Mercada, Noble, Niña, Oro, Palomba, Perla, Preciosa, Rosa, Rica, Reina, Señora, Sabia, Sol, Ventura, Virtud, Vida, Zafira, etc.

Let us also add: Calderón, Campos, Castro, Rodríguez, Zavarro and Pérez as family names.

They even introduced a special prayer in Spanish in their synagogues, and Bible passages are read in Spanish on holy days.

All wonderful and quite extraordinary! The lovely elegies and tearful jeremiads we recite on the Jewish day of mourning (the 9th of Av[15]), when we lament the destruction of Jerusalem, include one (whose author I cannot find now) composed in Hebrew and Spanish, which I include here as a curiosity:

"Yatzeu ahehem Ghezushim, Misheretz u-Mi-Sevilla
Raithi orpehem Cashim, Hevithi Gherush, Castilla
Ve-Sicilla, Aragon, Grenada." Olelay!!

Which briefly means, "The sad memory of the exile from the cities of Seville, Castile, etc., is considered like the exile from Jerusalem, though at the same time we acknowledge that both were by God's decree."

I mention this to show how much the Spanish Jews still love the cradle of their ancestors, who in their day were the glory of Judaism.

But how sad and bitter it is to love someone who detests you for no discernible reason.

---

[15] The Spanish edition mistranscribes this as "9th of April." Pulido's follow-up book corrects the error when quoting the same sentence.

Consider this beautiful, heartfelt declaration, expressed elegantly in the current Spanish of the Jews by a man of great authority, venerated for his wisdom throughout the East, the headmaster of one of the most important Spanish-Jewish schools, if not the first in its class, who has never visited Spain. He has no official or literary relationship to Spain or formal ties that would require or inspire such testimonials of gratitude and attachment. Such a letter is most worthy and vouches for the tenderness and veneration that these Jews retain for their adored homeland. It shows how highly they esteem her language, and the depths of religious humility and resignation with which they bear their banishment. They even place the loss of their sweet, dear Spain on the same footing as the loss of Jerusalem: a punishment from an all-powerful, righteous God.

For the moment, let us leave the estimable Mr. Bejarano, whose luminous expositions we shall revisit several times in these articles. Instead, let us turn to the important topic of preserving Spanish, and the regard in which Jews hold this language, as seen in other distinguished statements from the Hebrew people.

III

ON NOVEMBER 13, I gave a speech in the Senate that intrigued the Minister of State and roused his interest in this matter. A few days later, excerpts appeared in foreign periodicals more or less devoted to Jewish issues, and people mailed me clippings and letters. Some of this correspondence deserves publication, both for its content and for the Spanish in which it is written, which shows various levels of alteration from the mother tongue.

M. Gañy of Rosiori, Roumania, owns a huge insurance agency and a shop in partnership with a fellow countryman. On December 14, 1903, he wrote to me:[16]

> The Spanish people here were so pleased to read the request you made in the Spanish Senate.
>
> We speak Spanish and are well aware that our fathers are 400 years removed from those Jews.
>
> We preserve their language and many habits, but have no access to Spanish literature.

---

[16] Of all the Ladino correspondence in this book, his is the furthest from modern textbook Spanish. Here is a sample of his language as it appears in Pulido's book:

"Los españoles ke mos topamos aky, meldimos con grande plaser la demanda ke su osted izu en el Senado Español. Ablamos la lingua spañola y sabemos my boeno ke noestros padres si traban de los ebreos alongados agora 400 años. Guadrimos la lingua y muchos uzos, ma non podemos saber nada de la Literatura Spañola."

PULIDO'S NOTE: Meldar, a Judeo-Spanish verb: to read, to learn.

I imagine that Madrid must have an impartial literary journal, and I take the liberty of asking you to have an issue sent here to my address, as I wish to subscribe.

Sincerest regards.

I replied to this letter, enclosing a few periodicals.

Mr. Lázaro Ascher of Bucharest wrote to me on December 27:

As a lover of the Spanish language that I inherited from my parents and grandparents, which we still speak in my family, I am writing to ask if you could have someone send me the newspapers in which your speech appeared so I may read them in the original language?

I regret I was not here when you visited our city. I would have liked for you to see the students at our school for children aged 7 and above, who speak this lovely language of which it is rightly said, "It is the language for speaking to God."[17] Followers of our faith have translated all our prayer books, the Bible, and so on into the Spanish language. I only hope that someday I may have occasion to give you proof of my great gratitude and appreciation.

---

[17] PULIDO'S NOTE: An idea expressed by Bejarano, widespread among the Spanish Jews: Spanish is the language of God.

This same Mr. Ascher wrote again this year, on January 11, 1904:

> I lack words to thank you for your kindness in sending the extract from the Senate record containing your speech, encouraging propagation of the Spanish language. I never tire of reading it and my heart swells with happiness over your graciousness. Please accept my sincerest congratulations.
>
> As you rightly say, this will benefit international trade with Spain immensely, will foster this language among new generations, and will improve people's usage of a tongue widely spoken here and in the East among all the Spanish Jews.
>
> After so many centuries, of course, we have lost many words and replaced them with terms from our countries of residence. Some have degenerated (we say "filar" instead of "hilar" and "guadrar" instead of "guardar"),[18] but the large majority are unchanged.
>
> I am surprised to see that some Spanish authors use words of Hebrew origin such as "meldar" (from the Hebrew "melamed," meaning "scholar")[19] and "mazaloso"

---

[18] Pulido and some of his correspondents lament that in certain parts of the world, at the beginning of words, Ladino "replaces" the Spanish silent H with an F sound. In fact, the Spaniards' pronunciation is what changed: the initial F was once standard in Spain in words such as *fermoso* (now *hermoso*) and *facer* (now *hacer*), reflecting the words' Latin origins. The forms with an H were standard by the fifteenth century, but some Sephardim preserved the older form.

[19] According to the *Ladino-English/English-Ladino Concise Encyclopedic Dictionary* (2000), *meldar* ('to read') comes from the Greek μελετᾶν (*me-*

(from "mazal," meaning "luck"). Also the illustrious author Fernan Caballero says in The Seagull, in the story of Medio Pollito the half-chick, "And with these words he covered the spark with ashes, then began to crow according to his custom, as if he had performed a great exploit."[20] I know that this last word, "hazaña," means "great deed." But it seems to me "hazaña" must come from "hazzan"[21] (Hebrew for "cantor," the main officiant in a Jewish temple), which has been used in this sense since early times, and even in the Talmud the word meant "servant."[22]

These letters reflect love for one's native tongue, but also show the major alterations the language has undergone and the need to establish literary relationships that would be warmly welcomed. The correspondence above is, however, less important than the following letter from Mr. Daoud Rousso. This distinguished lawyer in Constantinople provides legal counsel to the Royal Spanish Consulate in that city. Mr. Rousso lays out, in elevated terms and with singular authority, the problem of Spanish in the East and the hazards of corruption it faces.

---

letan, 'to study'). *Meldar* is an everyday Ladino word, generally unknown in Spanish-speaking countries.

[20] Fernán Caballero (Cecilia Francisca Josefa Böhl de Faber), *The Seagull*, translated by Augusta Bethell, (London: Richard Bentley, 1867), vol. 1, 134.

[21] **PULIDO'S NOTE:** The Dictionary of the Spanish Royal Academy says that this word comes from the Latin *facimus*, 'action,' 'enterprise.'

[22] The Talmud uses the word *hazzan* in several ways. In connection with the ancient Temple in Jerusalem, the Talmud generally describes the hazzan as an assistant whose duties went beyond those that *servant* implies.

DAVID ROUSSO
LAWYER IN CONSTANTINOPLE, LEGAL COUNSEL TO THE
SPANISH ROYAL CONSULATE, ACTIVE IN JEWISH
COLONIZATION WORK IN PALESTINE

Its author wrote this in French, and we are publishing a literal translation of it.

It says:

Dear Senator:

My excellent friend vice-admiral Elías Pasha was kind enough to send me the transcript of the November 23 Senate debates. There I read your magnificent speech in favor of developing and improving the use of Spanish in the East.

This issue, which also matters greatly to the Eastern Jews, has long interested me. I therefore decided to send you a detailed study of the matter.

Spain does, in fact, have a treasure here worth exploiting, and it would take precious little effort.

A few years ago, some Judeo-Spanish periodicals campaigned insistently to replace the current jargon of the Spanish Jews with the national language (Turkish) or perhaps some other language of our own. For many reasons, I found this controversy completely at odds with the interests of the Eastern Jews. At the time, I did my utmost to defend the continued use of Judeo-Spanish, even in its current degraded state, in hopes of perfecting and elevating it later into a proper spoken language. My arguments prevailed then. However, we must recognize that the language as now spoken—moving further from its origins every day—could not hope to find much favor in the world. We must perfect it, improve it, infuse it with a form ever closer to the Spanish language. Today when an Eastern Jew speaks Judeo-Spanish, he in no way feels that he knows and speaks a beautiful living language as widely spoken as Spanish. Only by offering him ways to perfect and elevate his *patois* into a true language will he be able to grow fond of it and want to use his linguistic knowledge in international business. That is when Spain will truly have five hundred thousand new supporters almost without noticing. The matter seems urgent.

I shall be very happy to do anything I can to help restore the Spanish language in the East.

Feel free to contact me if I may supply further information.

I am mailing you a very curious booklet containing all the Spanish ballads sung by Jews in the East, as transmitted from generation to generation since 1492.

As sensitive as the memories of the past may be, the Eastern Jew loves his former country deeply and cannot forget her.

In turn, vice-admiral Elías Pasha, a Spanish Jew who holds a preeminent position in the Sultan's court and among Constantinople's medical professionals, wrote to me on January 26, also in French:

The issue you raise is unquestionably most interesting and needs consideration. We are talking about a population of more than half a million speakers of our pleasing language.

I forwarded the Senate Record to one of my friends, the lawyer D. M. Rousso, who knows the subject well, having addressed it often with great interest. In my opinion, it

is Mr. Rousso whom the Academy should name as a
member, as he could provide the needed services. Mr.
Rousso is also legal counsel to your honorable Consulate
in Constantinople, where he is much respected. He will
provide valuable services to the cause you are so fervently and intently promoting.

This distinguished doctor, whom I was honored to visit
at his home at Quatre Rues, in Pera, was one of the people
who most helped me to understand the danger of extinction Spanish faces in the East. As we chatted, I asked about
his family and he said he has children studying abroad. I
asked if they spoke Spanish and he said no: his children
were learning German and French. In other words, a family
that had retained its Spanish for four hundred years (Dr.
Elías Pasha speaks the Judeo-Spanish of the East, in which
we were conversing) is now cutting itself off from the native language of numerous generations of ancestors, and
educating its children in other tongues they doubtless consider more interesting and elevated.

This disquieting assessment of the future of their intimate language at Europe's eastern frontier was essentially
corroborated by Spanish Jews in other countries. They are
convinced Judeo-Spanish is basically a *jargon* (as they call it,
adopting a French word) and not a full-fledged language
that could suit the immediate demands of the human spirit
and international culture. Therefore, they hope to either
improve or replace it. This crisis in that race's destiny has
been addressed most firmly and clearly in places such as
Vienna. Numerous Spanish-Jewish students converge on

ELIAS PASHA
VICE-ADMIRAL, PERSONAL PHYSICIAN TO
HIS IMPERIAL MAJESTY THE SULTAN OF TURKEY

that capital: energetic, enthusiastic youths with faith and ideals, who can look to the future and undertake projects to maintain and strengthen their historical and ethnic identity, amid the growing battle in which nations absorb nations. To my knowledge, no one in our country has even discussed this grave question affecting the fate of a perennially exiled people, though this old motherland's language and nationality largely define the issue. We can find clear expressions of the matter in the charter of an organization called La Esperanza, and in a campaign by the newspaper *El Progreso*.[23]

The organization's charter, which I have in front of me, is written in Judeo-Spanish and German in two columns, and is dated July 24, 1897. Article 2 states:

> This strictly apolitical Society is designed to preserve the Spanish language and foster its members' scientific and literary instruction. It aspires to do this through appropriate readings with emphasis on Jewish knowledge and literature, through public discussions at the Society's meetings, by making newspapers and magazines available, and by starting a library.

This same fervor also led to the founding of the newspaper *El Progreso*, established in 1899 to defend the interests of Spanish Jews. Its issue of January 15, 1900 includes a remarkable manifesto from the board of La Esperanza, thor-

---

[23] The organization's name means 'Hope.' *El Progreso* was a Sephardic newspaper in Vienna, not to be confused with the Sephardic magazine of that title published in Adrianople, or with the Ladino newspapers called *El Progresso*, published in Constantinople and New York City.

oughly explaining the need to defend and improve the Spanish language.

This document, most of which appears verbatim below, would surely impress any good Spanish soul. Let us keep in mind that these are the words of the most enlightened Jewish youth, addressed to a people that settled not only in the Balkans but in most (or all) European countries and in parts of Asia and Africa. They insist that this fight to improve and thus preserve their ancestral tongue reflects no love for Spain: they pursue it for their own sake, to preserve their existence, and for the love of Judaism. This intriguing argument is justified by Spain's disdain for her former sons and daughters.

It reads:

Judeo-Spanish brothers.

[...]

La Esperanza, an academic Society of young Spanish Jews at institutions of higher learning in Vienna, aims to maintain and cultivate the Spanish language among its members. It therefore enthusiastically salutes "El Progreso" on its new appearance, smartly dressed up in the Latin alphabet. Since we love our nation's glorious past but fear for Judaism's fate and future in the East, our organization is forced to raise its voice publicly and state its convictions about the Spanish language and the change in "El Progreso"...

Hear, gentlemen! Listen, brothers!

Judaism in the Balkans has a thousand historical, national, ethical, moral and practical reasons to retain the Spanish language, that sturdy rope connecting all Jews of the East. Once this language is abandoned and forgotten, supplanted by our various countries' own languages, we shall no longer be a major branch of the Jewish nation but shall be chopped into tiny little bits, into fractions no longer able to understand one another, no longer feeling the blood of brotherhood that courses through their bodies. We shall be distant strangers. Unquestionably, uprooting our strength in this way would be a serious peril to Judaism, especially in an era when it is so urgent to make every effort to grow closer, to concentrate ourselves, to join hands in concord.

Therefore, not for the love of Spain, absolutely not, but out of love for ourselves, love of our existence and love of Judaism, we must SUSTAIN THE SPANISH LANGUAGE that our forefathers spoke and that we learned from earliest infancy as our native tongue!

However, the language we use contains abundant errors and flaws, mainly caused by writing in the Hebrew alphabet ....[24] others cannot be adapted fully to Spanish. This jargon, unsuited to science or literature, much less to making ourselves understood by each other and the world, this language without rules or scientific method is unworthy of advanced human beings who aspire to culture and education. This way of speaking .... foreign expressions and words that liken us to the Gypsies and distance us from every cultured nation, puts us in no position to express even one profound or abstract thought,

---

[24] **PULIDO'S NOTE:** These ellipses indicate text that was damaged on our copy. The reader can easily fill the gaps.

nor a single scientific or technical definition. This is why we Jews of the East have not produced and cannot produce men of literature or people of science. Without literature there are no noble thoughts, there is no idealism.

This is why our young people are moving away from our language, abandoning and forgetting it. Along with the language, they are also losing their Jewish feelings. So not for love of Spain much less for the sweetness of her language, but for love of our culture, of our advancement and future, we must PURIFY AND PERFECT our mother tongue!

This does not mean learning and purifying Spanish to the exclusion of our countries' national languages. Quite the opposite: since we are good, patriotic subjects of the country where we spend our lives, it is our duty to study and master her language. The former does not preclude the latter. We seek only to give up an error-laden jargon devoid of rules, and in its place to learn a methodical, rich and beautiful living language.

This is much simpler than we first imagined. "El Progreso" has already taken the first, most important step by using THE LATIN ALPHABET. This is practically all we need do.

In its new form, "El Progreso" will quickly:

1. help us turn our dead language into a methodical, scientific language;

2. take us from this desert in which we are languishing, and lead us into a broad, beautiful garden;

3. through reading, allow Jewish youth to purify and enrich our Spanish dialect, giving us the surest weapons for applying and achieving our nation's ideals.

At the end of this remarkable manifesto, the board of La Esperanza addresses every young Jew and every man and organization wishing to advance the Jewish people, and asks them to please participate in this pursuit as actively as possible.

That same issue of the newspaper, to show the difference between modern Spanish and the Spanish used by the Jews, also published three different poems. The first was a contemporary composition from Spain—combative, alive, restless, nervous, filled with grandeur—with footnotes explaining words that would be unclear or unknown to Jewish readers. By contrast, the other two poems were antique and outdated, and their language much closer to today's Judeo-Spanish.

Without further comment, let us turn our attention away from this campaign to revitalize Judeo-Spanish, launched by the young, cultured Jews who tread the classrooms of enlightened Vienna and pin their hopes and thoughts on a project vital to their national identity and to their Spanish community. Instead, let us see what our honorable friend Bejarano has to say about the state of the Spanish tongue. This headmaster of the Spanish-Jewish School in the Roumanian capital, an expert teacher of this form of Spanish, shares his thoughts about how Roumania's Jewish communities use it and the overall status of this serious matter, after summarizing how the language has changed in the four centuries since the Jews' exodus from Spain and Portugal.

Bejarano's observations also include comments of great interest to statesmen. He writes:

> These men (who took refuge in Turkey) produced multitudinous literary works, some published in Hebrew and others in a more or less ornate Spanish printed in rabbinical characters.
>
> That period gave us nearly 400 important literary works in Hebrew and 380 in Judeo-Spanish, mostly created by worthy men.
>
> Their texts address matters of theology, religion, poetry, astronomy, geometry, medicine and almost all the sciences of our time.
>
> Many, especially those in Hebrew, are astonishingly rich in content. Their laconic style demands rare intelligence to penetrate the author's meaning. Many of them required commentaries.
>
> Some of the works in Judeo-Spanish deal with science as well, but most are literature for the lay public: Biblical exegeses, morality, ethics, stories, pastimes, legends, maxims and proverbs.
>
> Incidentally, these books are so commonplace that the humblest people have some in their homes, and it is deemed a sacred duty to read them to one's family at night and on holy days.

It is true that over the past century, the language has decayed much, with an influx of jarring loan words and ill-chosen terms, but that is natural: dominant nations have a powerful influence on the language of any given people.

In the East, one can also find worthy manuscripts in Judeo-Spanish: collections of lovely anecdotes, sayings, rhymed verse, songs, and tales of yore. It is a true pleasure to hear them from the mouths of old gray heads.

In my last journey through those lands, I enjoyed studying these simple, gracious people. Each wrinkle on their faces seemed to me a fount of wisdom, a mine of knowledge.

It is from those good people that I collected some 2,000 proverbs, maxims, dictums, etc. for my study. I have been working on it for more than three years, writing the history of each saying and comparing it to those found among other peoples. God knows if they will ever see the light of day! There are not many options for publishing it!!

The beneficent atmosphere of the nineteenth century did much for the progress of the Spanish Jews. Seeing the usefulness of science, they aimed to shake off their lethargy and pursue a path of clarity. They lost some habits that were no longer beneficial and started to give their children a modern education, especially in the last fifty years, once the Alliance Israélite arrived in the East.

Goodness, what a change!! A whole new era opened for the Jews. The hundreds of thousands that it (the Alliance) spends on its schools bring the best results. It is a hygienic, scholarly, positive influence.

The creation of so many schools (that teach all the modern subjects, including Spanish) has produced delightful results. Through these houses of learning, the language has reached its apogee. People write correctly and speak with elegance and refinement, to the point where a Spanish gentleman arriving here will think he is in his own country. He would believe that our modern works of history, biography, etc. were by Cervantes or Calderón, so careful and fluent is the style.

My son, who imbibes his information directly from Vienna's Jewish community, says Bosnia is where young Jews speak the purest Spanish, or at least the most discerning Spanish since they try not to mix it with foreign words.

And since there are many interesting facets of this topic yet to explore, we shall continue in the next article.

IV

OUR PREVIOUS ARTICLE contained authoritative, up-to-date testimony and statements from Jews of Spanish descent, expressing the current state of their language in Turkey, Roumania and Austria-Hungary, three of their major population centers. To review the main points:

The Hebreo-Spanish people, dispersed across Europe, Africa and Asia Minor, are caught up in the turbulent, mighty, worldwide conflicts that seek to affirm certain languages and establish their dominance.[25]

Spanish Jews are convinced their household Spanish is deeply flawed and unsuited to the demands of public, international and national life.

This inferiority has led the race's most intellectual segments to argue persuasively that they must reform Judeo-Spanish—imbuing it with all the beauty, resources and advantages of an excellent, fully formed tongue such as contemporary Spanish—or else abandon their language and replace it with another.

Jews of Spanish ancestry, emerging from obscurity and from the modest social aims that typified their long, four-century exodus, are now scrambling to join the professional world in their countries of residence. They are storming universities and academies, invading the liberal professions and the most distinguished posts, and competing success-

---

[25] **PULIDO'S NOTE:** The Alliance Israélite Universelle, headquartered in Paris, is establishing schools everywhere and requires them to teach French.

fully against members of other races for jobs in all spheres and ministries: the military, science, politics, etc.

By virtue of this broader education, more and more towns now have Jewish schools of increasingly outstanding quality, in which the teaching of Spanish must vie with the teaching of other tongues, besides the country's own language.

The Jewish schools' Spanish classes receive no inspiration or aid or anything else from their old motherland. Instead, they drink their knowledge solely from the turbid, tainted, inferior, defective springs of antique Judaic books and of historical ballads, poems, fables, Bibles, exegeses, legends, etc. These cannot filter out the natural adulterants of their household language or encourage its natural, organic development.

After reading the personal statements in our last article, we may venture three more assertions:

Jews do not hold such bitter memories about their old mother Spain or such negative feelings toward her that they would systematically, passionately reject all guidance, aid and intervention she might see fit to dispense. They are hurt by the disdain with which they are viewed. However, when their poems, ballads and prayers speak of Spain, they always describe her as such a sweet, lovely country, so ideal and paradisaical. As for Spanish, whose altered state among them they acknowledge, they have a sublime opinion of this language "with which God speaks to the angels." Surely, any affectionate attention from the old mother country, however basic, would therefore be received with deep gratitude.

As evidence, I shall mention that a letter I received today (February 5) from my son in Vienna says:

> Yesterday (January 30), I was visited by a young man who is a former president of the student organization La Esperanza. He wanted me to ask the Ambassador if he would meet with him and if the Ambassador might accept an invitation to a dance the Spanish Jews will hold this month. I visited the Ambassador this morning and he told me that of course he will accept the invitation.

Even if Jews no longer feel true love for Spain, they might understandably tend to feel some respect and affection for her, despite everything that has happened. After all, nearly everywhere, Jews remain the exiled, persecuted people, and their miseries, past and present, attenuate the horrors and may calm any protests that historical wrongs and persecutions might inspire. If the Jews remember their age-old terrible afflictions, plainly these bring to their lips not complaints and ire but a resigned, sorrowful lamentation, which soon yields to hope of future reparations and much-deserved respect. Of the many Spanish Jews with whom I have spoken, only a merchant in Belgrade (a tobacconist near the Konak, whose shop we entered to buy postcards) expressed a harsh, resentful memory of the expulsion. This Jew of advanced years spoke heatedly, rejecting and offended by the idea of returning to Spain. His son, a fine-looking lad who was in the shop, listened silently with a smile, as if to say, "Why be so upset now over things that happened so many years ago?"

It can also be said that, in instinctive defense of their race and out of religious sentiment, Jews will try to maintain the Spanish language in their community records, declarations and documentation. It will, however, keep losing ground and prestige amid progress and as a result of changes in the Jewish home, as Jews seek better education for their children so they can meet the needs of their current social rise. They will continue to embrace Spanish only if they become convinced it is a useful tool that lets them communicate with the numerous Spanish-speaking nations: a language that, if used well (with all the sophistication, magnificence and beauty with which its mother country wields it), has no reason to envy German, English or French, and in some ways surpasses them. Only then will the Jewish people find Spanish attractive beyond its two historical purposes— racial identity and religious worship—and may cling to it out of usefulness and pride, crucial reasons not to renounce it in the name of modernity and innovative revolutions.

It is already declining in places such as Servia, where the king, Peter I, recently told the Spanish Jews it was a shame that they were abandoning Spanish, because it is an extremely beautiful language worth cultivating.

One last point: a perusal of Judeo-Spanish documents and treatises from throughout the exile shows that the language became disfigured and corrupted gradually as more and more time passed since the expulsion. In other words, Spanish Jews today write and speak worse than in the sixteenth, seventeenth and eighteenth centuries. Each day we see increasingly marked causes and effects of the degeneration that languages can suffer, as any living thing can, like an organism subject to a thousand nutritional and biological influences.

We have received two interesting recent Spanish-Jewish publications that prove this thoroughly: the *Dictionnaire Bibliographique des auteurs juifs, de leurs ouvrages espagnols et portugais* (Bibliographic dictionary of Jewish authors and their Spanish and Portuguese works) by the Hungarian scholar M. Kayserling, published in 1890, and *Recueil des romances judeo-espagnoles chantées en Turquie* (A collection of Judeo-Spanish ballads sung in Turkey) by Abraham Danon, director of the Rabbinical Seminary of Adrianople, from 1896. While reading them, one immediately notices very relevant lessons and healthy warnings about our topic.

First, though one book comes from the Hungarian capital and the other from European Turkey's largest city except Constantinople, and though the books deal mainly with Spanish literature, both are in French. The authors' acknowledgments mention information, inspiration and assistance from several countries, but mention no advice, references or aid from modern Spain. Kayserling dedicates his meritorious study to Steinschneider, an eminent bibliographer in Berlin. The author thanks Loeb in Paris and Davitcho in Budapest for summaries and useful assistance, and thanks the board of the Zunz Foundation in Berlin for funding publication of a book intended for "all those interested in the study of Spanish literature," with nary a thought to the nation and people that could and should be most directly interested in his work: the Spanish. [26]

The other lesson comes from Rabbi Danon, who, explaining why he wrote his study, fondly recalls hearing Spanish ballads as a child:

> Despite the pious care with which we tried to preserve [numerous ballads through the generations], a large portion of them were already lost by the time I was a boy, listening to my grandmother sing these sweet songs from our erstwhile homeland. I can still picture her with that faraway look, transported by distant visions, trying to reproduce half-faded harmonies with her voice, with her eyes, and even with her gestures. Is it my childhood memories that lend such penetrating charm to these songs, some of which are actually very mediocre? If my former enthusiasm has waned a bit, I confess I still feel deep respect for these remnants of the Jews' past in Spain, and I felt it my duty to try to save from oblivion what still survives. [27]

These thirty-five ballads that the Spanish Jews sing in Turkey may be mangled and disfigured, sprinkled with Persian, Turkish and Arabic phrases, and rife with interpolations, substitutions and omissions that render them obscure or even nonsensical. However, any Spaniard read-

---

[26] Kayserling, page v. Translated here from the original French.

[27] From Rabbi Danon's book, as serialized in 1896 in the Jewish scholarly journal *Revue des études juives*. Wherever Pulido diverges slightly from Danon's transcription, I have gone back to Danon for the Ladino. The rabbi's remarks were translated here from the French.

ing them would feel what Danon feels: echoes of early childhood, reverberations of eras past, a longing for the small villages and remote corners of old Castile, for the charm and childlike simplicity of a people's nascent folk poetry, of the legends and medieval rhymes our grandmothers told us, which rise in the soul like the dust and effluvia of venerated, long-gone ages.

One thinks instantly of Christmas celebrations and old, traditional Spanish carols when reading, for instance, these graceful, elegant rhymed couplets from ballad 34:

> Por ésta calle que vó,
> me dicen que no hay salida.
> Yo la tengo que pasar,
> aunque me cóste la vida.
> ----------
> Por ésta calle que vó
> echan agua, créce ruda.
> Esta la pueden llamar,
> la calle de las agúdas.
> ----------
> Ocho y ócho diéz y séis,
> veinte y cuatro son cuarenta;
> la móza que me quére bien
> déjeme la puerta abierta.

On this road that I travel,
They say there is no exit.
I must travel its entire length,
Though it cost me my life.

On this road that I travel
They throw water, and rue grows
It can truly be called
La Calle de las Agudas.[28]

Eight and eight are sixteen
Plus twenty-four makes forty,
O maid who loves me well,
Leave the door open for me.

It is odd to read the author's note speculating at length about the numbers in this verse, which he attributes to weddings lasting eight days and boys' being circumcised eight days after birth. Could we not more accurately attribute them to arbitrary numeric rhymes, found in our children's games and perhaps even in classroom exercises? After all, who does not remember this lyric, chanted thousands of times by our little girls in their singing game?

---

[28] *Calle de las Agudas* (or, in Catalan, *Carrer de les Agudes*) is a street name in Barcelona and other Catalan cities. In his French translation of the poem, Rabbi Danon renders this as "la rue des (dames) spirituelles": street of spiritual women.

Dos y dos son cuatro,
Cuatro y dos son seis,
Seis y dos son ocho,
Y ocho dieciséis,
Y ocho veinticuatro,
Y ocho treinta y dos,
Ánimas benditas
Me arrodillo yo.

Two and two are four,
Four and two are six,
Six and two are eight,
Plus eight makes sixteen,
Plus eight makes twenty-four,
Plus eight makes thirty-two,
Blessed souls
I kneel me down.

To give a sense of these ballads, we shall reproduce two of the shortest and best preserved. Readers may judge their close resemblance to old Spanish love ballads and see how, in all ages, writers used and even abused the rhetorical device of repeating the episode's main motif to invigorate the aesthetic impression (examples are legion, including the *Iliad* and *Odyssey!*), an approach modernists now use as if it were brand new.

ROMANCE XVII[29]

Arboleda, arboleda,
arboleda tan gentil;
en la rama de más arriba
hay una bolisa d'Amadi,
peinandose sus cabellos
con un peine de marfil,
la raiz tiene de oro,
la cimenta de marfil.
Par alli paso un caballero;
caballero tan gentil:
—Que buscais la mi bolisa?
que buscais vos por aqui?
—Busco yo á mi marido,
mi marido d'Amadi.
—Cuanto dabais la mi bolisa
que os le traigan aqui?
—Daba yo los tres mis campos
que me quedaron de Amadi.

---

[29] There are many versions of this ballad, often titled "Arboleda" or "Arbolera" ("Grove") or "La vuelta del marido" ("The Husband's Return," a title shared by several ballads). In some versions of this song, the woman sits on the smallest limb of a tree that has golden roots and ivory branches, tending her hair with a transparent or ivory comb. Sometimes, according to Rabbi Danon, the long-absent husband is not a knight or gentleman but a returning sailor.

BALLAD 17

In a grove, in a grove,
In a grove so fine;
On the topmost branch
Sits a lady married to Amadi,
Combing her hair
With an ivory comb,
Its handle is gold,
Its base, ivory.
A knight[30] passed by;
A knight so fine:
"What do you seek, my lady? [31]
What do you seek in this place?"
"I seek my husband,
My husband, Amadi."
"How much would you give, my lady,
To have him brought to you here?"
"I should give my three fields
Left to me by Amadi.

---

[30] *Caballero* can mean knight, nobleman, gentleman or horseman.

[31] *Bolisa* ('woman' or 'wife') seems related to the Turkish *boliçe* ('Jewish woman'). In his anthology, Rabbi Danon wonders whether *bolisa* came from an Ashkenazic pronunciation of the Hebrew בעלת-בית (*baalas-bayis*, 'lady of the house'), which would make it a cognate of the Yiddish בעל־הביתטע (*baleboste*). This appears unlikely, though, phonetically and historically.

PULIDO'S NOTE: A corrupted Hebrew word, equivalent to *señora*.

El uno araba trigo
y el otro zengefil,[32]
el más chiquitico de ellos
trigo blanco para Amadi.
—Mas que dabais, la mi bolisa,
que os lo traigan aquí?
—Daba yo mis tres molinos
que quedaron de Amadi.
El uno molia clavo
y el otro zengefil,
el más chiquitico de ellos
harina blanca para Amadi.
—Mas que dabais, la mi bolisa,
que os le traigan aquí?
—Daba yo las tres mis hijas
que me quedaron de Amadi.
La una para la mesa,
la otra para servir,
la más chiquitica de ellas
para holgar y para dormir.

---

[32] **PULIDO'S NOTE:** Arabic: ginger.

One grew wheat
And the other ginger,
And the tiniest of all,
White wheat for Amadi."
"What else would you give, my lady,
To have him brought to you here?"
"I should give my three mills
Left to me by Amadi.
One ground cloves
And the other ginger,
And the tiniest of all,
White wheat for Amadi."
"What else would you give, my lady,
To have him brought to you here?"
"I should give my three daughters
Left to me by Amadi.
One to set the table,
The other to serve,
And the tiniest of all,
To dally and to sleep."

—Dádos á vos, la mi bolisa,
que os le traigan aqui.
—Mal año tal caballero
que tal me quijo decir.
—Que señal dais, la mi bolisa,
que os le traigan aqui?
(—Bajo la teta izquierda
tiene un benq maví[33])
—No maldigais, la mi bolisa,
yo soy vuestro marido Amadi.
Echados vuestro trenzado,
me subiré yo por allí.»
(Tomaron mano con mano
y se fueron á holgar.)

---

[33] **PULIDO'S NOTE:** A Turkish word: it describes a blue blemish.

"Give yourself, my lady,
And he shall be brought to you here."
"Fie on you, knight,
For saying such a thing."
"What sign will you give, my lady,
To have him brought to you here?"
(Below her left breast
She has a blue blemish.)
"Curse not, my lady,
I am your husband Amadi.
Throw down your braid,
And I shall climb up there."
(They took hands
And went off to dally.)

ROMANCE XXII

Levantime, madre,
un lunes por la mañana;
me lavi las mis manos,
tambien mi linda cara.
Me asenti en la ventana,
vide pasar un mancebico,
alto era como el pino.
Se lo demandi á mi padre
que me lo diera por marido.
Mi padre, por no descontentarme,
presto atorgó conmigo.
Lo demandi á mis hermanos
que me lo dieran por marido.
Mis hermanos, por no descontentarme,
presto atorgaron conmigo.
Lo demandí á mi madre
que me lo diera por marido.
Mi madre por no descontentarme
presto atorgó conmigo.
A la entrada de la puerta,
me pareció un cirio encendido.
A la subida de la escalera,
me pareció un cirio florido.

BALLAD 22

I arose, mother,
One Monday morn;
I washed my hands,
And my lovely face.
I sat in the window,
And saw a lad walk past,
Tall as a pine.
I asked my father
To get him for my husband.
My father, not wanting me to be sad,
Quickly agreed.
I asked my brothers
To get him for my husband.
My brothers, not wanting me to be sad,
Quickly agreed.
I asked my mother
To get him for my husband.
My mother, not wanting me to be sad,
Quickly agreed.
As we entered the door,
I saw him as a glowing candle,
As we climbed the stairs,
I saw him as a burning candle.

A la entrada de la sala
me pareció una almenara.
A la entrada de la cama,
me pareció un viudo entendido.
Si se lo digo á mi padre,
me dice: tu te lo quijites.
Si lo digo á mis hermanos,
me lo toman por mal hadádo.
Si se lo digo á mi madre,
luego se mete á llorar conmigo.
(Ahora, por mis pecados,
me lo llevo yo conmigo.)

As we entered the room,
I saw him as a blazing candelabrum.
As we entered the bed,
I saw him as a knowledgeable old widower.[34]
If I tell my father,
He says, "You wanted him."
If I tell my brothers,
They say it was unlucky fate.
If I tell my mother,
Then she starts weeping with me.
(Now, for my sins,
I carry him with me.)

---

[34] In footnotes, Danon and Pulido mention an alternative version of this line: "Me pareció un mal tendido," the meaning of which is not entirely clear, even to people who study medieval ballads.

The colleagues I consulted generally agreed that it is a pun on *malentendido* ('inexpert person,' 'misunderstanding'). Beyond that, they proposed interpretations ranging from criticism of the groom's sexual inadequacy (imagery of drooping laundry posts or of clothes flopping in the breeze) to mockery of his unimpressive appearance (comparing him to a badly worn bedspread or a poorly made bed). One colleague even read *mal* as a noun and *tendido* as an adjective, making the groom "a troublesome thing, stretched out."

At the end of Kayserling's previously mentioned Dictionary, he publishes a series of Spanish adages or proverbs that the Jews use, and instantly one sees their pristine Spanish lineage. We still use many of them today. Here are some of the less well known:[35]

On friendship:

> *Quien no da migas no tiene amigas.*
> She who never serves *migas* has no friends.[36]

> *Si tu enemigo es una urmiga, contalo como un gamello.*
> If your enemy is an ant, when you tell the story make him a camel.

> *Un corazón espejo de otro.*
> One heart is the mirror of another.

---

[35] For these sayings and for the song at the end of the chapter, this English edition relies on Kayserling's books for the Ladino text whenever there are discrepancies with Pulido's transcription.

[36] *Migas*: a traditional spiced bread-based dish in Spain. The saying means that people must give of themselves if they want friendships.

REFRANES

ó

PROVERBIOS ESPAÑOLES

DE LOS

JUDIOS ESPAÑOLES

ORDENADOS Y ANOTADOS

POR

Dr. M. KAYSERLING.

BUDAPEST,
IMPRENTA DE SR. C. L. POSNER Y HIJO.
A COSTA DEL AUTOR.
1889

TITLE PAGE
KAYSERLING'S COLLECTION OF "SPANISH ADAGES OR
PROVERBS OF THE SPANISH JEWS," PUBLISHED AS A
SEPARATE VOLUME IN 1889.

On love:

> *De mi quieres? á ti quiero, hay grande diferencia.*
> Between "Do you love me?" and "I love you," there is a
> great difference.

> *Quien quere á la rosa, non mire al espino.*
> He who loves a rose must ignore the thorns.

On stubbornness:

> *Derroca una pared, para avanzar un clavo.*
> He would knock down a wall to drive a nail.

> *Quien tiene colcha y no se cobija, no es de agedear.*
> A person who has a quilt but won't use it deserves
> no pity.

Axioms:

> *Del espino sale la rosa, de la rosa sale el espino.*
> From the thorn comes the rose, from the rose comes
> the thorn.

> *Mas vale un asno que me lleva, que un caballo que me echa.*
> Better a donkey that carries me than a horse that
> throws me.

Quien vende el sol, merca la candela.
He who sells the sun must buy candles.

*Tres cosas feas hay en el mundo: rico mentiroso, pobre
gabiente, y viejo putañero.*
There are three ugly things in the world: a lying
rich man, a haughty poor man, and a whoring
old man.

Boca dulce abre puertas de hiero.
A sweet mouth opens iron doors.

Cara alegre, dos candelas.
A happy face is as bright as two candles.

El gamello vee solo la corcova de otros, y no la suya propia.
The camel can see others' humped backs, and not
his own.

Mas vale caer en un rio furiente, que en la boca de la gente.
It is better to fall in a raging river than into gossiping
mouths.

Deja tu casa, ven á la mia, verás un buen día.
Get out of your house and come to mine, and you will
have a day that's fine.

Quien mi vee mi goza, quien mi tiene mi llora.
Seeing me is a pleasure; having me is a tragedy.

Leon que esta dormiendo, no lo espiertes.
Don't wake a sleeping lion.

No hables mal del dia asta que no anochese.
Don't speak ill of the day until the sun has set.

Si negra la culpa, mas negra la disculpa.
The darker the guilt, the darker the excuse.

Mas tura un tiesto roto que uno sano.
A broken pot lasts longer than a whole one.

No miercoles sin sol, ni viuda sin dolor, ni mochacha sin amor.
There's no Wednesday without sun, no widow without
grief, and no girl without love.

El bostezo va de boca en boca, como el vino de bota en bota.
A yawn travels from mouth to mouth, like wine from one
wineskin to another.

And so on.

Of the extremely famous or very common sayings, we
shall cite just a few:

Dame gorduras, te dare hermosuras.
Show me fat and I'll show you beauty.

El comer y el arrascar, es todo al empezar.
Eating is like scratching yourself: once you start, you
can't stop.

Cuando crecera á la rana pelos.
When frogs grow hair.

El cantaro va al agua, asta que non se rompe.
If the pitcher goes to the well often enough, it will break.

A ti te lo digo mi hija, que lo entienda la mi nuera.
I'm telling you this, my daughter, so that my daughter-
in-law will hear it.

Camina con buenos, te haceras uno de ellos.
Walk with good people and you will become one
of them.

Quien tiene techo de vidro, no eche piedra onde el vecino.
People with glass roofs shouldn't throw stones at their
neighbor's house.

And so on.

The printed page cannot convey the severe transformations the Jews' Spanish has undergone. The changes are still more extreme in the spoken language: certain letters (such as Y and J) no longer sound the same, and the vowels I and E are used in ways that are confusing to us.[37]

Kayserling tells us that after their banishment, those first Jews cultivated Spanish literature very well. This is why the treatises, tracts, legends, etc. they published in those days possess a clean, elegant expression that sometimes rivals that of our most graceful, careful writers of the 1500s. The descriptions and titles in Kayserling's bibliography prove this convincingly. Later, though, the language deteriorated and became corrupt: The lexicon changed because many terms were replaced by words from languages such as Hebrew, Persian, Turkish, Arabic, French and Italian. The exact value of prepositions shifted. Gender and number agreement became debased, as did the grammatical system. The music and majesty of the era were lost, and it all fell into pitiful barbarism. Well-educated Jews preserved the language in some countries, including Italy, the South of France, and Holland, where it was widely published. In the East, however, a jargon soon emerged, a sort of vernacular commonly known as "Ladino" or "Ladino Spanish," a term

---

[37] As noted before, some language traits that Pulido considers eccentricities of Ladino were, in fact, once standard Spanish. Other differences came from writing Ladino in the Hebrew alphabet (using just one letter to transcribe both E and I, for example, and just one letter for O and U). Still other differences arose through normal language-change processes: metathesis (transposition of adjacent letters or sounds), simplification of consonant clusters, adoption of loan words, etc.

that, according to Rosanes of Rustchuk, comes from *latino,
latinar, ladinar.* Translating into Spanish was and is called
"meldar en ladino," literally "reading in Ladino."

In this *Ladino* jargon, even a word's structure often
changed: some gained an M or N (*amvisar* instead of *avisar,
munchos* instead of *muchos*) and others transposed letters
(*vedre* for *verde, pedrer* for *perder*).

On top of this, Jewish authors use numerous variant
spellings. For instance, among proper names, we find
Yshac, Ishac, Isac; Moseh, Mosse, Mosé; Aboab, Abuab and
Abohab.[38] In addition, women in the East—who, as everywhere, handle most of the child rearing—did not like to
read. Combine these factors and you will understand perfectly the linguistic decay seen in the deformation of every
prosodic element and of every grammatical dynamic and
grammatical mechanism of their speech.

Still, using this relatively contaminated Ladino, Jews in
Belgrade, Constantinople, Salonika, Smyrna, Bucharest and
elsewhere publish newspapers, ordinances, regulations,
bulletins and religious documents, and it remains the everyday language of Eastern Jews. As Kayserling put it, no
language has managed to supplant a country's native
tongue entirely except Spanish, beloved by Jews across the
centuries.

We shall conclude this article by reprinting a song that
combines Hebrew and Spanish words:[39]

---

[38] This list comes from Kayserling, *Biblioteca,* v.

[39] **PULIDO'S NOTE:** סׁישיר נאמן (Amsterdam, 1793); see *Orient* (1844)
p. 683, reported by A. Ink (pseud. of A. Jellinek).

Vendra el Señor de la redencion[40]
A decir á todos: vamos a Zion
בשורות טובות esperemos nos vendran
A poco, a poco, se sentiran,
אליהו הנביא se aparecera,
para alustrar á hijos de Zion,
   ya vendra etc.

De las cuatro partes nos acogera,
á ירושלים venid! nos dira,
iremos diciendo nueva שירה
Cantar de los cantares que á Zion,
   ya vendra etc.

---

[40] Pulido copied this song and its citation from Kayserling, *Biblioteca*, xx.

The Lord of redemption shall come
To tell everyone, "Let us go to Zion"
Let us hope that [41]בשורות טובות will come to us
Gradually, they shall be heard
[42]אליהו הנביא will appear,
to purify the children of Zion,
    He shall come etc.

From the four corners He shall gather us,
Come to [43]ירושלים! He shall tell us,[44]
we shall go singing a new [45]שירה
A song of songs saying that to Zion
    He shall come etc.

---

[41] **PULIDO'S NOTE:** Good tidings.

[42] **PULIDO'S NOTE:** The prophet Elijah.

[43] **PULIDO'S NOTE:** Jerusalem.

[44] The rhyme scheme spans both languages: the Ladino *dira* ('shall tell') rhymes with the Hebrew שירה ('song') in the next line.

[45] **PULIDO'S NOTE:** Song.

De aqui en poco luego sera
que á todos los muertos avivara,
todos los אומות se levantaran
para ir á ver á hijos de Zion,
    ya vendra etc.

Ya vendra Moseh el pastor נאמן,
que por su זכות decendo מן,
y agora presto vendra el זמן,
de rescatar á hijos de Zion,
    ya vendra etc.

It will not be long now
Until He revives all the dead,
all the [46]אומות shall arise
to go see children of Zion,
He shall come etc.

Moshe the [47]נאמן shepherd shall come,
whose [48]זכות brought down [49]מן,
And now the [50]זמן is coming soon,
to rescue children of Zion,
He shall come etc.

---

[46] Nations. (Pulido's note here says "people.")

[47] **PULIDO'S NOTE:** Faithful.

[48] **PULIDO'S NOTE:** Virtue.

[49] **PULIDO'S NOTE:** Manna.

[50] **PULIDO'S NOTE:** Time.

V

OUR TASK IS NEARLY DONE. Obviously, even by writing an overview and omitting much crucial evidence and substance, we could not fit our topic into four articles. Two more remain. How could we end without looking at the current social importance of those who, calling themselves children of Spain and brothers to her native children, share our ties to a once great and now unfortunate nation? How could we end without mentioning at least some of the steps we think the Spanish government and certain national institutions should take for the good of the country and her reputation?

On seeing the title of our studies, some readers may dismiss the topic as trivial or even scandalous. Yes, such attitudes still exist. The world has seen much social progress in the past two centuries, and the spirit of brotherhood and religious tolerance has made possible such sublime evangelic gatherings and events as the World's Parliament of Religions in Chicago, which sparked Castelar's enthusiasm and led him to praise it in the most beautiful and sublime terms, even by his superlative standards. But certain people, in their fanaticism, ignorance or unthinking responses, consider the Semitic people, in all its branches and nationalities, as merely a Christ-killing race and a horde of rag-clad, filthy, grasping merchants who would commit any atrocity, even murder, for a few gold coins. Did we not just see and hear a plain example in the last few days? (We mention the incident as a curious case of social psychology, with no desire to offend.) This involved a member of the Congress of Deputies: a Republican lawmaker who, given his natural political leanings, generally embraces and embodies democratic feelings and the spirit of tolerance, and even supports reparations to races once persecuted and abused for religious and sectarian reasons beyond any individual's control. Nonetheless, this same man, seeking to upbraid the prime minister, shouted in Parliament, "Let that *Chueta* keep speaking!"[51] He thus used and, in his way, revived a slur that is one of the most unjust, abominable holdovers from the old battle between the races, which still endures *somewhat* in the idyllic, welcoming land of Majorca.

Over time, our requests for information have produced copious responses, and we have consulted numerous works from different parts of the world to see what they say about the current status of the Jewish people. Much of the material consists of reports on and responses to the persecution they suffer in revolutionary France, more cruelly in Russia, and today mainly in Roumania, and we could write something truly interesting about this aspect of Jewish life. However, lest this draw our attention disproportionately

---

[51] Xuetes (*Chuetas* in Spanish) are descendants of a group of Majorcan Jewish families that converted to Catholicism during the worst years of the Inquisition, but who maintained a distinct cultural identity and community. For hundreds of years, the term *Xueta* was used as an insult, though it has been rehabilitated somewhat since then.

Well into the twentieth century, Xuetes were regarded with scorn by some Gentile neighbors, who saw them as not quite Christians and not quite Jews.

from our topic, we prefer to focus on the information gathered in our travels and especially the facts supplied by our honorable friends, as our aim is to promote a more elevated, honest view of Spanish Jews than people generally have.

As we noted already, the Jews banished from Spain can now rival the other social classes in nearly every country in Europe, Asia and Africa where they live. Like people of other heritages, they participate in the military, universities, the press, laboratories, industry, commerce, legislatures, banking, law, medicine..., everywhere, promoting the splendor of intellectual life, the advance of progress, the always-sublime epic story of civilization. They are spreading the moral doctrine and the practice of redeeming the humble, aiding the needy, relieving the afflicted, and in general improving the lot of unhappy humanity, and they perform this mission with the same inescapable passions and frailties as members of all races, all peoples.

What is more, their own race still considers Spanish Jews to be favored by a long-acknowledged ethnic and social selection. In his history of the Jews of the Ottoman Empire,[52] M. Franco reminds us what the histories of this misfortunate people say on the subject: that the Jews of Spain—especially those from Catalonia, Aragon, Navarre and Leon—together with those from Portugal, known collectively as *Sephardim*, were considered a race superior to their brothers the *Ashkenazim*, who come from Russia, Germany and Austria. They believed their number included

---

[52] M. Franco, *Essai sur l'histoire des israélites de l'Empire Ottoman depuis les origines jusqu'a nos jours* (Paris: Librairie Durlacher, 1897).

direct descendants of the family of King David, a nobility and distinction that all the others acknowledged.[53] Given this, and because their long immersion in Spain and her culture had schooled them in the teachings, comforts and gifts of a stable, ordinary life, their banishment was all the more terrible than the exile of people accustomed to lifelong hardships, insults, abuse and adversity.

My son writes to me that the Spanish Jews are more respected in Vienna than those of German origin. The latter, because of their manners and history, are seen as *parvenus,* while the former have the pride of their past, their consequence, their stability. As a curious aside, people say that even when Spanish Jews express anger or have fits of passion, they do so with greater refinement. Their bodily appearance is also distinctive: they have traits they acquired on Spanish soil, and their women are of such celebrated beauty that, in Vienna, they have a well-established reputation as the prettiest women in that lovely, aristocratic capital. "I didn't see even one ugly girl there," my son tells me, referring to a Spanish-Jewish dance he attended recently, "and I was surprised at the singular beauty of their dark eyes, only comparable to the most seductive of our Murcian and Andalusian girls."

As they do in Vienna, people in other nations also prize the beauty of Spanish-Jewish women. As proof, we recall

---

[53] Some eighteenth- and nineteenth-century Ashkenazic intellectuals idealized Sephardic culture and medieval Sephardim. See, for example, John M. Efron, *German Jewry and the Allure of the Sephardic* (Princeton: Princeton University Press, 2015).

that Carroll Spence, a U.S. government minister who served in Constantinople, published an article in 1870 in the *Baltimore Saturday Night* about the status of Hebrews in the capital of the Ottoman Empire. He wrote:

> The descendants of Spanish Jews in Turkey have light complexions and often red hair; as a race they are well formed, with intelligent faces. Their women are among the most beautiful females in the East. Their blue or gray eyes and fair complexions contrast most favorably with the dark eyes and raven locks of their sisters, whose ancestors inhabited more eastern climes. Their language is a sweet Spanish patois.[54]

The list of renowned Jews who influenced the intellectual and material progress of humanity is long. For sixteen centuries the Hebrews have never stopped working. Leven could have mentioned many other glorious Israelites when he recalled Saadia, Maimonides, Judah Halevy, Mendelssohn, Graetz and Munk as benefactors and geniuses of times past. We Spaniards can never sufficiently lament having made it impossible for us to claim the likes of Spinoza, who could have made us proud and benefited us just as Lord Beaconsfield[55] and Lord Rothschild did for England (Lord Beaconsfield had the same ancestors as the celebrat-

---

[54] The article he quotes is C.S., "Roumania and the Israelites: The Israelites in the Ottoman Empire," *Baltimore Saturday Night*, June 25, 1870, 1. According to Pulido, C.S. was Carroll Spence, who served as U.S. envoy extraordinary and minister plenipotentiary to the Ottoman government in the mid-nineteenth century.

[55] I.e., Benjamin Disraeli.

ed Camondo family of Constantinople, of Spanish-Portuguese origin);[56] just as General Ottolenghi and the economist Luzzatti did for Italy; just as Millaud, Gambetta, Hausmann and Loevy did for France; and just as Ballin, Bleichroder, Fustenberg and Goldberger did for Germany. Most of them distinguished themselves as heads of government ministries or of great scientific, administrative or financial institutions. We say they could have made us proud and benefited us because today, the Jewish communities of Spanish ancestry still shine in their intelligence, education, industry, healthy patriotism, and love of family.[57] Their creations and literary renaissance, especially in Constantinople, mark them as worthy descendants of those illustrious, brilliant authors of literature and treatises who, in Amsterdam, Ferrara, Venice, Padua, Antwerp, Frankfurt, Salonika and many other cities, proved their great intellec-

---

[56] **PULIDO'S NOTE:** After the expulsion, this family settled in Venice, where many of its members became famous for their knowledge and for service to their new country. They then moved to Constantinople where Count Abraham de Camondo, "the Rothschild of the East" (1785–1873), was born. He died in Paris at his mansion on the Parc de Monceau, leaving behind a fortune of 125 million francs. He had arranged for his remains to be taken to the famous cemetery at Haskeuy, whose white stones are reflected in the liquid mirror of the Golden Horn. (*Essai sur l'histoire des israélites de l'Empire Ottoman.* Franco.)

[57] **PULIDO'S NOTE:** In Tangier, in Tetuan and in all the towns in Morocco where the Jews speak Spanish, men consider women their equals: a woman eats at her husband's table, receives visitors, does the household bookkeeping, comes and goes, laughs and speaks with complete freedom. (*Bullet. de l'Alliance Israélite,* 1903, page 109.)

TRANSLATOR'S NOTE: The journal citation above is incorrect.

tual energy, rich stores of knowledge and strong work ethic. Such assets constitute the most august grandeur of nations.

It is an undeniable, glorious fact that the emigrants from Spain and Portugal advanced printing and publishing considerably with their Hebrew and Judeo-Spanish books. That is why Salonika, Constantinople and Smyrna had printing presses soon after that marvelous device's invention, two hundred years before the Turks used them. It is also common knowledge that the Jews' dispersion across the world gave them facilities and skills for the banking business; that among them, there was a proverbial dictum that Spanish mothers in the East would recite to their children to urge them to study:

> Escribe derecho, derecho, techo con techo
> y te harás yazidi del comercho;

> Write clear and fine in a straight line
> And you shall become a Yazidi of commerce.[58]

It is also well known that medicine, jurisprudence, music, philosophy and literature were liberal professions in which Spanish Jews shone with indisputable, much vaunted supe-

---

[58] Yazidis are a Kurdish religious and ethnic minority who lived in many parts of the Ottoman Empire but are now concentrated in northern Iraq. Over the centuries, they have been frequent targets of violence and intolerance.

In a parenthetic note here, Pulido says that Ladino uses the word *Yazidi* figuratively to mean 'scrivener.' I have been unable to confirm this.

riority. Perhaps the medical field did include some rabbis who were exorcists and Kabbalists who treated patients with psalms and incantations, but they were outnumbered by illustrious, brilliant professors of medicine whose wisdom and accuracy surpassed Turkey's doctors of Christian, Armenian, Greek and other extractions.

It would be historically inaccurate to hide their periods of steep decline, as this race was always terribly beaten down and persecuted by exclusionary laws, humiliating prejudices, horrific accusations, and violence, fanaticism and fear. Such prejudices destroyed their property, robbed their wealth, murdered their men and violated their women. Even legal threats, law enforcement and the protection of sultans often could not deter this pernicious fate. Therefore, among their lower social strata, one could always find (and can still find) the destitution, squalor, neglect and indifference of a race subjected to many centuries of cumulative, intense despair. Even so, when reading their history, one realizes that these Jews could say, like most people, that they have done more than enough by just surviving, by avoiding such numerous, obstinate, frightening causes of annihilation. Spanish Jews held eminent positions in the Turkish imperial court in the sixteenth and seventeenth centuries but lost much ground in the eighteenth century, when they lost almost all their positions in government and the professions. They rose again in the nineteenth century thanks to decrees from sultans such as Mahmoud II, Abdul Medjid, Aziz and Hamid, and their grand viziers. With paternal feelings and noble tolerance, these leaders sought to equalize the rights of all their subjects: they defended the Hebrews against bloodthirsty enemies among the Arabs, Turks and Orthodox Christians, granting positions, appointments, honors and commissions to Spanish Jews. This let them travel once more down the road of progress, again overtaking much of the lead that other nations in the Empire had gained over them, especially the Armenians and Greeks. This put them in a position to benefit from the highly effective educational programs of powerful, capable Jewish organizations and associations such as the Alliance Israélite Universelle, the Jewish Colonization Association and the Anglo-Jewish Association.

These institutions' schools have spurred an extraordinary recovery, and we can affirm that Jews today are radically changing their historical personality. A new race is emerging: well educated, with broad horizons and a strong, powerful mental and cultural constitution; a race ready to reconquer its civil rights and its social standing through achievement in fields different and more distinguished than those that, throughout their history, their race seemed destined to embody forever. European education in the East has been so successful that, as early as 1889, the Alliance's *Bulletin Annuel* reported yearly expenditures of more than seven hundred thousand francs on education, and years later it could be said that a hundred thousand Ottoman Jewish men and women knew French as well as they knew their country's own Turkish tongue.[59]

---

[59] **PULIDO'S NOTE:** By the end of 1902, the Alliance was operating 118 schools, educating thirty thousand children.

Franco has detailed the great progress in educational practices. We Spaniards of the West would do well to learn about them for many reasons, as they define the transformation occurring among the Spaniards of the East.[60]

In the eighteenth and early nineteenth centuries, education was generally limited to the following: Boys attended a *maestra* (nursery school) run by a woman, and then went on to a *Talmud-Torah* (primary school) with as many as sixty pupils, taught by one male teacher called a *señor haham*.[61] In this room, the boys were divided into groups seated on the floor in a circle, called a *havurah*, around the teacher. Each group learned a different topic: the first studied the Hebrew alphabet; the second, Hebrew vowel points; the third, spelling; the fourth, reading proficiency; the fifth, translation of the Bible into Judeo-Spanish; the sixth, translation of the Commentaries of Rashi (a twelfth-century French rabbi); the seventh, the reading of pious texts in Judeo-Spanish, such as the *Meam Loez* and the *Kav ha-Yashar*; and the eighth, the eldest group, learned the basics of the *Talmud*, Judeo-Spanish cursive handwriting, known as *solitreo*

---

[60] Pulido lifted the next three paragraphs nearly verbatim from pages 261–62 of M. Franco's *Essai sur l'histoire des israélites de l'Empire Ottoman* (1897). Pulido translated the French passage into Spanish and occasionally condensed or paraphrased the wording.

[61] *Haham*: Hebrew for 'wise.' By extension, in Ladino it means 'rabbi.' According to Franco, the larger Talmud-Torahs in the Ottoman Empire were typically one-room schools with as many as five dozen boys sitting in circles on the floor, grouped by age. One rabbi taught them all, wandering from group to group.

(literally "isolated letters," from "solo-letero"), as well as addition, subtraction, multiplication and division.

Students remained in these classes from age seven to age thirteen, after which they went to a four-year *Yeshiva*, or upper school. Lastly, boys went into business or prepared to become rabbis.

Nowadays, by the end of their five years in school, Jewish students can read and write Judeo-Spanish, Hebrew and two or three modern languages: French, Turkish, Arabic or English. They have a basic grasp of world history, with emphasis on Turkish and Jewish history; geography, physiology, hygiene, zoology, botany, mineralogy, physics and chemistry; arithmetic with whole numbers and decimals; commercial calculations, currency, weights and measures; the rules of interest, currency exchange, etc.; penmanship, drawing, geometry and algebra.

Thus provisioned with the most abundant, useful weapons for life's battles, they are transforming the dignity and character of the Hebrew people appreciably.

They are now aware of their civil rights and civil liberties, and of the protection that the imperial government grants them. They communicate extensively with people of other faiths. Hygiene, now taught at school, is changing their repugnant appearance. They dress in the European style, and the women are on a par with their husbands in terms of general knowledge and in the tastefulness of their headwear and hair. The old, nauseating Jewish ghetto is giving way to the beautiful requirements of modern urban planning. They are less religious in their behavior and external relations, and therefore more open to compromise, more sociable, and less exposed to theological disquisitions and the dangers that used to arise from them. Unlike past generations, they no longer face scorn, hatred or censure from fellow Jews for studying foreign languages, for being freethinkers to varying degrees, for eating at Christian or Moslem tables, for missing religious services, and so on, and they no longer marry very young or cower and hide in their Jewish quarters and their synagogues.

They produce a great many periodicals, and the printing houses of Vienna, Belgrade, Constantinople, Salonika and Smyrna issue numerous Judeo-Spanish books: not only Bibles, moral discourses, and excerpts from the *Zohar*, but also grammars; Hebrew-Latin glossaries; books on history, geography, astronomy and arithmetic; biographies of celebrated Jews; novels in translation; science books; and so on and so forth.

This is why Sultan Adbul Hamid, like many of his predecessors, has shown them his appreciation. Jews occupy an honored place in his court, even more so than they always did. Jews have been esteemed courtiers in Turkey since the exodus from Spain brought them to Constantinople with an element of culture and knowledge that Sultan Bajazet praised and vouched for with the famous quotation that appeared in our second article.

It is estimated that more than a thousand Spanish Jews hold high-ranking posts in the Turkish government: generals, colonels and captains; doctors, surgeons and pharmacists; members of the High Council; and noted essayists and journalists. According to the numbers we have received, Turkey has one Spanish Jew in the Municipal High Council, fourteen in the Ministry of State, two in the Ministry of War, three in the Ministry of Commerce, three in the Ministry of Postal and Telegraph Services, two in the Ministry of Public Education, six in the Ministry of Imperial Education and in the military and civilian schools... among many others.

Spanish Jews are at the forefront of Ottoman commerce, and some are millionaires. As Bejarano told me, "If Spain had negotiated and encouraged the repatriation of these Jews, I can think of a few who would have brought with them more than a billion francs. We are not talking about admitting poor petty thieves, but rich, enterprising people."

According to him, right in the city where he lives, Bucharest, several businesses acquire manufactured goods and other wares from Barcelona, and are satisfied with the prices and quality of the Spanish merchandise.

We have said that Spanish Jews have a very active press, and it is true. Judeo-Spanish periodicals, established over the past sixty years, are legion. The first, a Turkish publication founded in Smyrna in 1846 by Rafael Uziel Pincherte under the title *Sha'are Mizrach* or *Puerta de Oriente*,[62] preceded

---

[62] Editor Rafael Uziel and frequent contributor Isaac Pincherle (not Pincherte) were, in fact, two separate people.

Sha'are Mizrach (Hebrew for 'Gateway to the East,' co-titled *Puertas del Oryente* toward the end of its run) is the earliest known Ladino newspaper. It published at least seventeen issues in Smyrna from December 1845 to November 1846. The paper shut down because of insufficient subscriptions. See the detailed discussion starting on page 31 of Olga Borovaya,

a long list of titles from different cities. Examples include *La Luz de Israel, El Nacional, El Tiempo, El Progresso, El Telégrafo, El Sol, El Amigo de la Familia* and *El Instructor* in Constantinople; *El Lunar, Salónica* and *La Epoca* in Salonika; *La Esperanza* and *La Verdad* in Smyrna; *El Dragoman, El Nacional, El Correo de Viena, La Política, Illustra Guerta de Hestoria* and *El Progreso* in Vienna; *El Lucero de la Paciencia* in Turnu Severin, Roumania; *El Amigo del Pueblo* in Belgrade, Servia, etc., etc. Such periodicals have earned their illustrious writers well-deserved fame, though only in Jewish circles because of their harmful habit of publishing entirely in rabbinical characters. We shall discuss some of them in our next and final article, for we have already exceeded the bounds of a well-proportioned essay.

Modern Ladino Culture: Press, Belles Lettres, and Theater in the Late Ottoman Empire (Bloomington: Indiana University Press, 2012). The book also reproduces a page from issue 12 of this newspaper.

Uziel's plans for an earlier Ladino paper in the same city, *La Buena Esperansa*, fell through for financial reasons in 1842. A successful Ladino paper of this title began publishing in Smyrna in 1871.

VI

READERS WHO WERE benevolent enough to read our first five articles will understand why we feel the need for this final one, containing proposals on the topic. For how could we declare the subject closed without first venturing a few suggestions meant to open up relations and achieve useful areas of influence?

To reiterate essential points that we should never forget or ignore: We must remember, day in and day out, that prudent, well-run nations fight tirelessly to expand and strengthen their international influence, and that one way to do this is by spreading their language. Spain's recent calamities have cost her so much that was of value, and she must now search everywhere for new infusions to make up the losses, in order to increase and develop her diminished riches, energy and global prestige. The actions of England, Germany, Italy and France prove that a nation's reach extends wherever its language goes. We still have a perfectly rational, positive chance to extend our intellectual sovereignty: in exchange for fair reparations, we can obtain the goodwill, affection and precious linguistic tribute of a hardworking race that has shown unparalleled historical loyalty, and which is spread over so many nations of the civilized world and the East. Wasting this opportunity would reflect peerless incompetence and the most pathetic shortsightedness. In five or ten years, Spain would find that other nations have benefited by claiming what we once had and failed to appreciate. It is a strange, reprehensible fact that while France, Germany, England and the United States encourage the teaching of Spanish in their schools, granting it the same standing as other languages needed for social interaction and competition—which they do to further their own speculative goals—Spain has not stopped to think of such things. We are not even taking the steps that would demand the least effort, sacrifice and energy.

The world has handed us an ideal strategic situation: more than half a million families[63] abroad consider themselves Spanish, and romantically call themselves our siblings or children. They sigh for Spain and choke up with ineffable tenderness when they invoke and recall her natural beauty. They deem her long-ago loss an inconsolable tragedy, equal to the loss of Jerusalem. These families— motivated by religion, preserved traditions, an emotional link to legends and ballads handed down through the ages in the sanctuary of the home, and by a practically organic heritage, perhaps strengthened and preserved by their endless misfortunes—are predisposed to venerate their legendary motherland. They are likely to show deep gratitude for any affectionate interest and attention our government might dispense. If the other party (meaning us) neglects its obligation to provide reparation and appreciation—which it could grant while still profiting from the situation—and if it fails to seize this chance with the proper attention and generosity, that failure should be condemned as a colossal hapless blunder. Such outrageous, censurable ignorance

---

[63] Here again, the nearly half a million Sephardic Jews cited earlier have somehow become more than half a million families.

would befit a nation that has steadily lost the sources of her legendary greatness, only because she lacked the judgment to appraise events and interests with that sense of reality that all well-governed countries need.

Therefore, we shall propose a way to avoid further historical remorse and additional great loss, addressing four national bodies that we consider obligated to act: the Ministry of State, the Academy of the Language, the Chambers of Commerce, and the Association of Writers and Artists.

Let us take these one by one.

What has our Ministry of State or any governing body done, in all these centuries, to learn about and appeal to this multitude of Spaniards around the globe, after confessing the harm their expulsion has caused us? To our knowledge, nothing. We angrily hurled the Jews from our land with the Catholic Monarchs' famous edict of March 31, 1492. The Hebrews scattered chaotically, as best they could, in the four months allotted (no later than the end of July, it said), fanning across Europe and Africa, with most traveling to the East to seek the protective, self-serving tolerance of Bajazet II. There and everywhere, they continued to love Spain, study her literature and language, and show signs of civic integrity, industriousness, humility and intelligence. We, in turn, never glanced at or studied them again— neither as an ethnic curiosity nor as a literary matter—nor did we send any attention or appreciation in their direction. Later we did condemn and express regret over the inept edict, but we have never done anything about it. They were left with the pain of their woeful banishment, and we with the memory of our absolute intransigence. That is where things stand: neither side interacts with or even knows the other, perhaps because we seemingly hold the same mindset and attitudes as 412 years ago, or rather because any sea change in ideas and circumstance has not led to appropriate action.

Leave religious motives aside: let each race and people live with its own religion and then, within that categorical statement, let each individual follow the faith that suits him. Spain passes for a zealously Catholic country, but a truthful census of her residents' consciences would surely yield a result very different from her public image.

Let us also set aside the fantastical notion of mass repatriations of the exiles: this is impractical and the Jews would not leave the countries where their interests lie, which also hold the ashes of generations that lived there for four centuries. That is enough to sanctify the ground of their current homelands with venerated memories.

On both these central issues, we can—and should—make two crucial points.

One is that Spain today tolerates and respects all religious practices, as must any civilized nation that venerates human rights. It is true that our major cities of Madrid, Barcelona and Seville are not as cosmopolitan as Paris, London, Berlin, Vienna or Constantinople. In those foreign locales, the Greek church with its splendor and dazzling ornamentation, the synagogue with its Eastern architecture, and the Protestant house of worship with its austere sobriety stand side by side with the Apostolic Roman church. Together they form a unit of brotherhood and tolerance that is, in itself, the most sincere, beautiful prayer that could ever extol the shared father of the entire misfortunate, suffering human race. Not so in Spain, thanks to our non-cosmopolitan character. Spain is, however, now home to many Evangelical chapels that pursue their faith in peace and safety, protected by our constitutional law. If these exist, then so could other religions' temples, whichever they may be.

The second point is that in 1881, the then Minister of State, the illustrious Marquis of Vega de Armijo, made the government's position clear in response to Russia's ferociously medieval persecution of the Jews. Six years later, Prime Minister Práxedes M. Sagasta reaffirmed that message in Congress when answering a question from the Republican legislator Eduardo Baselga, on the afternoon of February 11, 1887. Both statements made clear that any Jews wishing to live in Spain would find a tolerant, welcoming nation here. Under articles 2 and 11 of the Constitution of the Spanish Monarchy, they would enjoy full civil rights with no exclusionary laws, oppression or abuse of any kind. This is probably not well known among all Spanish Jews, who may suspect that the clergy still run our governments and that the sinister figure of Torquemada still looms over people's fates. Our fevered, often tactless political campaigns bolster this impression. The fact is that today's Spanish culture and laws would not allow any administration, no matter how reactionary, to violate the sacred freedom of religious conscience. Like the Inquisition, this belongs to the past. Spain's borders are open to her former children, as they are to everyone. The famous edict of Ferdinand and Isabella has expired, revoked by later laws. A Spanish center for Jewish immigration opened in Madrid on December 30, 1886, with the Hon. H. Guedalla of London as its honorary chairman, Mr. Lapuya as its president, and the participation of others. It was not a success but there is nothing strange in that, nor is there reason to analyze the natural causes of its demise. What matters is that today, Jews can easily become Spanish citizens if they wish.

In the Senate, I asked the Minister of State to have his consuls gather statistics on the population size and geographic range of this race. I also asked him to give preference to its members when appointing consuls in the relevant countries, and to let them know Spain considers and esteems them as her children. These attentions would cost us nothing and would always be appreciated, such as perhaps selecting some of them for honors or decorations. This would be enough to sow good seeds in their minds, which are fertile ground, and then reap ample harvests of gratitude and loyalty, which would only be to our profit.

I also asked the Royal Academy of the Language to join this enterprise. To my knowledge, the Academy has never taken any actions to collect, study or notice current Judeo-Spanish literature or the acclaimed Spanish-Jewish essayists and journalists. I suggested they honor some of these by naming them corresponding members, institute prizes to encourage Ladino authors, and work to uplift their language and bring it closer to our own. That august Academy's most recent yearbook (from 1903) lists the names of its full members, followed by its corresponding members in Spain and abroad. None could be considered Eastern European except maybe Father Körosi Albin of Budapest, and the Hungarian capital barely counts, as it is more properly in Central Europe. The Academy has ninety corresponding members, including many in every country of South America and nearly every European nation. But there is not one in the lands where Judeo-Spanish is spoken and where there are Judeo-Spanish schools, journalists and so on. This confirms the complete lack of suitable relations between the body in charge of preserving and spreading our language and the many famous Spanish-Jewish writers who are published in Spanish in Constantinople, Salonika, Smyrna, Bucharest, Vienna, Budapest, Adrianople and similar big cities.

Many of these writers, no doubt, deserve and would appreciate such an honor, and this would help to initiate exceedingly useful relations. A few paragraphs and a short speech by someone as humble as me was able to inspire poignant correspondence with honorable people in distant lands. How much more might the illustrious Spanish Academy of the Language accomplish by paying attention to them and encouraging this project?

Let me mention some names. First, a man whose fame reaches here from the East, where I first heard of him: the illustrious journalist, essayist and distinguished educator, David Fresco. According to Franco's *Essai sur l'histoire des israélites de l'Empire Ottoman*, Fresco's books and newspapers are so popular in Turkey that no Jew is more famous in the East, from the shores of the Bosphorus to those of the Danube, and along all the coasts of the Archipelago and of the Mediterranean. His newspaper, *El Tiempo*, was considered a model of professionalism, variety, and use of the Judeo-Spanish language. It has been said that "it is written in such a pure style that, if you transcribed the articles from rabbinical characters into the Latin alphabet, many could bear comparison to those of a Spanish newspaper." His biography, which we cannot publish here, is notable; his intellect was evident from a very early age; his contributions to Jewish culture are extraordinary; his writing in the press and in books was prolific and sound; his literary style is highly celebrated for its tenderness, delicacy and wit; and some of his works are already classics.

Second, we mention Enrique Bejarano, widely published in periodicals in Germany, Galicia (the Austrian Galicia), Jerusalem, Constantinople, Bucharest and Bulgaria, and even in the Spanish press. A teacher of Spanish at a school he directs in the Roumanian capital, he has a passionate, lyrical style, written with appealing affection and grace. His linguistic knowledge is extraordinary, as one might expect of a man who knows many languages. He has a rich, unpublished collection of ballads, maxims, tales, etc. gathered over several years among the communities of the East, and it would be commendable if the Academy were to publish it for use as a Jewish literary textbook.

Another deserving figure is David Rousso, a lawyer in Constantinople and great expert in Eastern Spanish, who played a large role in defending that language from proposals to abandon it. He is praised as an illustrious practitioner of the literary arts by such scientific eminences as Elías Pasha, physician to the Sultan, in a letter we have published.

This distinguished Hebrew is actively involved in the Jewish colonization of Palestine, to which he travels frequently.

Aaron Joseph Hazan of Smyrna, publisher and editor of *La Buena Esperanza*, is descended from an eminent family. He made his mark writing about religious subjects.

Sadi Levy of Salonika is the publisher and editor of the newspaper *La Epoca*.[64] This learned, hard-working person has done much to elevate the cultural level of the Spanish Jews in a city where that race abounds and predominates as nowhere else, accounting for 60% of the census.

Abraham Danon of Adrianople, director of the Jewish Seminary of Constantinople, wrote the booklet of old Spanish ballads discussed in our previous articles. This well-known, erudite scholar founded *El Progreso*, a magazine in Adrianople that debuted in 1888, to publish documents

---

[64] By the time Pulido's article was in print, Saadi Halevy (1820–1903) had died and the newspaper was in the hands of his son, Sam Lévy (1870–1959). Sam modernized and expanded *La Epoca* and went on to found and edit Sephardic periodicals in other parts of the world.

Father and son each left behind a memoir, both available in relatively recent editions: Sa'adi Besalel a-Levi (tr. Isaac Jerusalmi), *A Jewish Voice from Ottoman Salonica: The Ladino Memoir of Sa'adi Besalel a-Levi* (Stanford: Stanford University Press, 2012) and Sam Lévy, *Salonique à la fin du XIXe siècle: Mémoirs* (Istanbul: Isis, 2000).

about the history of the Eastern Jews. He has published a *Revue des études juifs* and other nonfiction works of great interest.

Also noteworthy are Rabbi Elías Crispín, born in Stara Zagora, Bulgaria, who published *El Luzero de la Paciencia* in the Latin alphabet;[65] Mr. Samuel Elías, who did the same with the *Amigo del Pueblo* in Rustchuk; and Mr. A. Capón of Sarajevo, Bosnia, who published *La Alborada*. All three have achieved well-deserved literary fame.

Mr. M. Franco, one of the Alliance's distinguished, conscientious teachers, published a remarkable work in French in 1897 about the *History of the Jews of the Ottoman Empire from their Origins to Our Days*, a valuable, extensively documented book. Also, young Mr. Salomón A. Rosanes, so knowledgeable about the history of the Spanish-Jewish people, has published a French-language biography of his renowned family and a study on the Spanish Jews of his country. He is reportedly preparing a well-documented study on Spanish Jews in general.

Besides these celebrated literary figures, we should cite other famous names such as the aforementioned Elías Pasha, personal physician to His Imperial Majesty the Sultan, honored with the First Class Order of the Osmanieh, First

---

[65] Born in Bulgaria around 1850, Rabbi Eliahu M. Crispin (fl. 1870s–80s) fled to Romania during the Russo-Turkish War. From 1885 to 1888, he edited one of the era's few Ladino periodicals printed in the Latin alphabet: *El Luzero de la Pasensia*, published in Turnu Severin. He used Latin letters reluctantly, out of necessity, since he did not have access to Hebrew type. Some sources give his first name as Eliyahu or Elias, and some spell his last name Crespin.

Class Order of the Medjidie, and the gold and silver Imtiaz medals; Isaac Pasha, vice-admiral, health inspector of the Ottoman Navy, president of the Central Consistory of the Jews of Turkey, a man to whom the Sultan entrusted many important missions and whom foreign sovereigns, and even Abdul Hamid himself, decorated with many distinguished orders; Colonel Moisés dal Medico, another famous writer of treatises; Pinhas Asayag of Tangier; the learned teacher Moisés Fresco of Galata, from whom we have received interesting correspondence; and many others whom, under other circumstances that allowed more space, I should be very happy to present to the Spanish public.

Does the Royal Academy of the Language think it could not start an exchange of important ideas, writings and correspondence with these people? Would that lofty organization lose something by naming them as corresponding members and engaging them in the patriotic task of regenerating their language and creating grammar texts and suitable books? Could it not see fit to underwrite and sponsor courses in Spanish?

The Association of Writers and Artists also has a fine chance to toil productively for the glory and benefit of Spanish letters. Some of the Jews are curious about Spanish literature, with which they are entirely unfamiliar. Books reach them in every European language but ours. I sent a compendium of the Academy's Grammar to a distinguished, pretty young lady in Vienna, and a French-Spanish dictionary to a wealthy agent in Roumania, at their request. We also sent novels, poetry and periodicals to various locales, and all of this generated interest and

ISAAC PASHA MOLHO
PHYSICIAN TO THE SULTAN OF TURKEY

recognition. Why not try to conquer that audience for our literary market, which is already somewhat developed among Spanish Jews in Morocco? The Unión Ibero-Americana does wonderful, patriotic, productive work promoting relations between the Americas and the Iberian Peninsula. Why not pursue similar work with our Spanish Israelite brothers, who live closer and may be easier to engage?

Lastly, the Chambers of Commerce should realize the potential benefits of regaining the friendship of the most commercially successful, most widely dispersed race in the world. If these organizations are worth anything, can foresee anything and have enough vision to look beyond our borders (and we believe that they are and they can), they will not view such a matter with indifference.

And that is quite enough!

To conclude, I thank *La Ilustración Española y Americana* for the warm welcome they have given these articles. I could have taken them to several magazines, but I believed a topic of this nature deserved a proper exploration in this publication: the pride of our fine arts and the prize of our literary world. Our most illustrious, glorious contemporary writers have graced these cultured, clear, distinguished columns with their creativity and patriotism. What other magazine could be so appealing and tempting to the eye and intellect of the Spanish Jews themselves? Might not its splendid, praiseworthy pages also serve to stir in them pleasant memories of the beautiful country where it was printed?

In a letter from February 15, Bejarano writes that the first of my articles, published in *La Ilustración*, made him, his wife and their children weep when they heard it read and pondered sweet recollections of a lost country. What greater reward for my humble work! What a sublime recompense for a publication dedicated to the pure exaltation of the Spanish soul!

[2]

Letter to
La Esperanza

Published in the Madrid newspaper *El Liberal*,
February 17, 1904.

To the President and members of La Esperanza,
the Spanish-Jewish Society of Vienna.

Dear kind compatriots:

My son, a doctor taking specialist courses in Vienna,
sent me word of your organization and some documents
explaining your noble aspirations to sustain and regenerate
the Spanish language that your ancestors spoke here in
Spain in the late 1400s, when they suffered their woeful exodus. Later generations of Jews, who spread into France,

Holland, Italy and especially Turkey, stayed faithful to this revered language that you seek to preserve and must therefore regenerate. This launches you into today's febrile contest among languages that are fighting for dominance in most cultured societies. That battle threatens to eliminate a language that for four centuries linked Jewish communities across many lands: your spiritual language for communing with God in your synagogues, a language that was the soul of the family for sacred and sweet interactions at home.

I have read your Society's charter, which says that your main goal is to *"preserve the Spanish language and foster its members' scientific and literary instruction."* I also read your eloquent, ardent Manifesto from January 1900, burning with the sacred flame of love for your race and your historic nationality, published in *El Progreso* in Vienna and addressed to all your brothers in the Balkan nations and principalities. Aiming high but with due caution, you rightly urged a joint effort to regenerate your speech with elements of modern Spanish, to assemble *"a methodical, rich and beautiful living language"* that meets all the scientific and literary needs of modern culture. You exhorted your fellow Jews to abandon that *"error-laden jargon devoid of rules"* into which your Spanish had deteriorated through the profound corruption caused by four centuries of suffering, persecution and banishment. Reading it touched me deeply as a Spaniard, and nearly all my countrymen would feel the same if they were to see it. How could anyone who loves his native country not feel overwhelmed by emotion and gratitude for your race's laudable general efforts, which you young students embody with such a magnanimous sense of community? Who could help but admire this latest reflection of your lingering fond devotion to the *"sweet, divine* motherland" that you consider lost, "like Jerusalem, because of decrees on high"?

Through this Society, you young people gathered in Vienna (natives of different lands, pursuing erudite, advanced university and professional studies) certainly prove yourselves worthy representatives of a race that always showed its love of learning. Your people never held grudges against our unhappy country, which long ago confessed that one of its worst, most hurtful errors was its inability to resist the wild fanaticism of that era and treat you as useful, enlightened offspring of its glorious soil.

Yes, your love of education is clear. Amid the apocalyptic ill fortune and horrors you suffered, it is well known you deployed no other defenses and sought no remedy but school and study. Even in our times, when your most famed, energetic benefactors arrived on the scenes of unutterable disasters, they stayed true to a defining trait of your people: no matter where fate led Israel's wanderings, and no matter where Israel paused to rest her broken body, you immediately created schools that were open to Jews and your neighbors, regardless of their religion. These benefactors did the same. It is what Crémieux and Munk did when, called to Damascus in 1840, they saw the life-threatening poverty of the Jews in Egypt, and set up schools in Cairo and Alexandria. It is what good Picciotto did in 1859 when, called to Morocco to observe the devastation caused by an epidemic, he considered schools the most effective way to meet vital needs. The Alliance Israélite Universelle took the same approach when, in 1862, two years after its founding, it visited North Africa and established its first school in Tetuan, and then another in Tangier, and then many others in Tunisia, Algiers, Turkey and Persia. These quickly served as first drafts of the schools your people have since founded in Rishon-le-Zion near Jaffa and in Samarin near Haifa, through the generosity of Edmond de Rothschild; and also in Jerusalem and in Mikveh,[1] which is to say, in that Palestine of which you retain such dramatic, venerable memories and in which you always place such pleasant, consoling hopes; in Djedeida, where rich Tunisian harvests flourish and ripen; and in many other places, including Paris itself, where your school in Auteuil trains teachers of both sexes to spread its teachings to Jewish schools around the world. Your educators even teach in the United States,

---

[1] The pioneering Mikveh Israel agricultural school and farming colony will figure prominently in later sections of this book. The AIU established the school in 1870 along the Jaffa-Jerusalem Road. The sultan had granted the school some seven hundred acres of government land free of charge for ten years, after which the Alliance would have to pay rent. According to the *Jewish Encyclopedia* (published over the course of several years in the early 1900s), the AIU originally hesitated to establish the school because "many members of the Alliance doubted the adaptability of the Jews to agricultural work."

Pulido's mention of "phalanxes of emigrés" to the U.S. is also a reference to the AIU. When he wrote this book, the Alliance was the main organization coordinating the emigration of Jews fleeing violence and oppression.

the new Promised Land, where you have brought phalanxes of emigrés who are constantly leaving behind the injustices of European nations. Many of these emigrants were forced out by tumultuously horrific persecutions, such as those that demolished every Jewish community in Russia in 1881, from Yekaterinoslav to Vilna,[2] through pillage, arson, destruction and death. Given this focus on education, no one could doubt the venerable Mr. Leven's statement last spring, at the most recent Assembly of the Alliance Israélite: that all Jews were always literate enough to read their Bible.

When I say you profess an inextinguished adoration for this legendary motherland of yours, it is because I have seen and heard it from Jews both illustrious and humble, when traveling down the Danube or shopping at stores in Belgrade, Servia; when visiting synagogues and schools in Bucharest, Roumania; when studying the hospitals and medical schools reflected in the lively waters of the Bosphorus and the Golden Horn in Turkey; when receiving heartfelt, affectionate letters and dispatches from Jews who, from opposite ends of the map, express adoration for this old Castilian soil, which, like you, has been wounded and battered by misfortune.

Hail to you, the brilliant Spanish-Jewish youth of Vienna: I salute you, I praise your effort to regenerate the language of your elders, and I hope you will be crowned with success.

---

[2] In the original, "de Ekaterinaslaw a Vilna," as if to say "from A to Z."

Yes, I salute you personally and on behalf of millions of Spaniards, who will feel paroxysms of gratitude when they learn that in far-off lands, there are throngs of upright, learned, industrious people who call themselves Spanish and who, after four centuries of exile, still extol the beauties of their language and the charms of their lost homeland with a litany of tender, loving phrases. By contrast, within Spain, countless native Spanish sons mistreat and abuse each other every day. I fervently entreat you to retain your sublime sentiments for many years to come.

Never renounce this lovely Spanish tongue, and defend it against invasions from other languages. Spanish is used and disseminated by many advanced, cultured nations, where Spain once expended her age-old riches and energies. No language can surpass its beauty and phonetic resources. To echo our great Castelar, who was the divine incarnation of its grandiloquent potential, this language is the greatest creation of the Spanish mind: no other is as imperial in its varied, intertwined roots, in its numerous and harmonious sounds, in its musical onomatopoeia, in its melodic sweetness and thundering vitality, in its unearthly rhythms and cheeky informality, in its well-proportioned distribution of vowels and consonants (which firmly distinguishes it from both the hardness of German and the melopoeia of Italian), and in the delicate scent left on it by Celtic and German, Greek and Latin, Arabic and Hebrew... All those languages adorned it with their inlays and enamels and garlands, with their shades and resonances, with their bounteous and congenial lexicon, thus making Spanish—as your poets and prose writers put it, with hyperbolic intuition—the means of expression with which *God talks to His angels.*

Would you like to know it well? I promise to send you, very soon, many modern Spanish books for your library, surely including some with inscriptions to you from their authors. These can be part of the reading and learning with which you hope to regenerate your impure Ladino language.

With an embrace, and warm regards from your old mother country,

Dr. Ángel Pulido,
Senator representing the University of Salamanca

On February 23, my son, young Dr. Ángel Pulido, read that letter to members of the organization to which it was addressed, producing an enthusiastic response. They agreed to answer it on the Society's behalf in publishable form.

True to my word, I have begun collecting books from distinguished Spanish authors, who, spontaneously or upon request, generously sent them inscribed. If I receive assistance from the Ministry of State, as promised by the current minister, Mr. Rodríguez San Pedro, I shall send the shipment in a few days.

As I write this, the following have already contributed copies of their works: Mrs. Emilia Pardo Bazán, Mr. Juan

Valera, Mr. José Echegaray, Mr. Benito Pérez Galdós, Mr. Joaquín Dicenta, Mr. Ramón Menéndez Pidal, Mr. F. Navarro Ledesma, Mr. Alfonso Pérez Nieva, Mr. Carlos Groizard, Mr. Manuel Tolosa Latour, Mr. Nicasio Mariscal, Mr. Ezequiel Solana, Mr. Armando Palacio Valdés, Mr. José Rodríguez Carracido, Mr. Eduardo Lozano and his wife Mrs. Luciana Casilda, Mr. Eusebio Blasco, Mr. Felipe Pérez y González and Mr. Rafael Altamira.

[3]

Jewish correspondence

BELOW ARE SOME OF THE letters we received in connection with these initiatives of ours. All were addressed to the author personally, but we are nonetheless publishing them (with apologies to their kind writers). We do so because they all contain proposals, opinions, sentiments, protests and information, some curious and some interesting, that illustrate our topic. Some, like those from Messrs. Bejarano and Ascher, bear a stamp of intimacy we fervently requested, to take our examination into the sacred space of the Jewish family, always conceived of in Spain as highly moral, but not well known in our culture. We reproduce this correspondence scrupulously, preserving its style and spelling.

Two letters precede it: one from that masterly author Mr. Juan Valera, and another from Spain's learned Chief Customs Officer, Mr. Juan B. Sitges, because they address the same purpose as the other letters.

Juan Valera

The Hon. Ángel Pulido.

Dear sir and distinguished friend:

I have read the articles you have been sending me and also the ones you have been publishing in *La Ilustración Española*.

It would be desirable, certainly, for the Eastern Jews of Spanish descent to study and speak Spanish as they once did: without the intrusive archaisms and foreign words they now generally use, but as it should be spoken and written, as it is spoken and written today on our Peninsula.

Your effort is very patriotic and, if successful, may prove very useful to those of us who write in Spanish, opening a new market for our works, spreading our fame and improving our earnings.

I am, however, saddened because I suspect that such Jews—especially those in Vienna and other cities of the Austrian Empire—have no strong, practical desire to study the language of Castile and perfect their use of it. It would be so easy for them to obtain Spanish books if they wished. They need only contact booksellers in Paris, Madrid or Barcelona, who would happily send however many they might order.[1]

---

[1] **Pulido's note:** Spanish Jews, in general, do not read the Latin alphabet we use. (See the letters from Mr. Sitges on page 123 and Mr. Fresco on page 187.)

I shall still join the effort and echo the idea that we must go to the mountain if the mountain will not come to us.

It therefore pleases me deeply to send you two of my books to send to the Esperanza Spanish-Jewish Association of Vienna or to wherever you deem fit.

In one of them, *Morsamor*, I discuss the Spanish Jews when they were expelled from Portugal and Spain, and in the other, *Garuda*, I refer to the story of a Viennese Jew of Spanish descent, and I praise that segment of the Hebrew people. I am sending you two copies of *Morsamor* and a dozen of *Garuda*.

I shall be pleased and flattered if these two books of mine are read and esteemed by these descendants of our former countrymen. As you know, they love the country they were forced to leave and they love her language so much that they still speak it today, though in an antiquated, somewhat corrupt form.

I remain your affectionate colleague and good friend,

Juan Valera.

JUAN B. SITGES

THE HON. ÁNGEL PULIDO.

My distinguished friend:

Health problems and too much work delayed my congratulating you on your beautiful Senate speech of November 13 about the Jews of Spanish origin living in the East, who speak Spanish that is archaic and often incorrect, but understandable enough to hold long conversations with them, as you and I have both done.

The surprising thing is that those Spanish-speaking Jews cannot read Spanish written or published in the ordinary alphabet, but only in rabbinical characters. They publish a number of newspapers in these Hebrew letters, of which I can recall *El Telégrafo* and *El Tiempo* in Constantinople, *La Época* in Salonika, *La Esperanza* in Smyrna and *El Amigo del Pueblo* in Sofia.

As a result, very few people in the East have read books or periodicals from Spain, and exceedingly few in Spain know or are aware of what little is published in rabbinical characters in those countries.

Setting aside any religious ideas, it would be most advisable to try to establish relations with the Spanish-speaking Jews, so as to extend Spain's trade and culture. I tried to do this years ago, with little success. My overtures received a chilly, polite reception from some, and scant sympathy from others.

You have been more fortunate and achieved much with your outstanding speech. You convinced the Count of San Bernardo, our Minister of State at that time, to say he would consider setting up schools in foreign locations that have large concentrations of Spanish speakers, even if they are Jews, to keep alive the principle of the beautiful Castilian language.

That is precisely where to start, and it would not even require what the Minister of State proposed. We need not *establish* special schools: it is enough to create teaching chairs in existing Jewish schools, to teach students a little grammar and how to read Spanish in the conventional alphabet.

Clearly this will require textbooks, but these will be neither voluminous nor costly. Publishing a Spanish-to-Rabbinic vocabulary will take little time and effort.

If we did this, the benefits of such education would appear quickly. Perhaps the first would be a market in these countries for our delightful works of literature, past and present, now completely unknown to the Spanish-speaking Jews.

You have pondered where to establish teaching chairs, and you therefore asked people to prepare statistics on the Eastern Jews.

A cursory estimate already exists. At my request, Spain's current ambassador to Portugal, Mr. Polo de Bernabé, kindly had one prepared when he was in charge of the Commerce Division of the Ministry of State. The archives of that division should still have an excellent report signed by Mr.

Antonio de Zayas in Constantinople, dated August 15, 1897, regarding the social, political and commercial status of the Hebrews in three countries: the Ottoman Empire, the kingdom of Roumania and the principality of Bulgaria.

Mr. Zayas estimated that 52,000 Spanish-speaking Jews live in Constantinople, 50,000 in Salonika, 22,000 in Smyrna, and lesser numbers in many other municipalities. These are, I think, underestimates and incomplete. The main problem with the numbers given annually in *The Statesman's Year-book* is they do not distinguish between Spanish-speaking and non-Spanish-speaking Hebrews.

The East is not the only place with Spanish-speaking Jews. It is common knowledge that many live in Morocco. Less well known, though you have publicized the fact, is that they exist in Austria, especially Vienna. In 1888, to mark the rebuilding of an old Synagogue there, an *Historia de la comunidad israelita española de Viena* (History of the Spanish-Jewish community of Vienna) was published in German and in a Spanish version in rabbinical characters, prepared by Rabbi Miguel Pappo.[1]

What is more, some live in Spain as well, not even counting those in Gibraltar. Not many years ago, Seville's indus-

---

[1] Rabbi Michael Papo prepared the Ladino half of this bilingual booklet. Adolf von Zemlinszky, a journalist who had served on the board of Vienna's Sephardic Community, composed the history in German under the title *Geschichte der türkisch-israelitischen Gemeinde zu Wien von ihrer Gründung bis heute nach historischen Daten* (History of the Turkish-Jewish community of Vienna from its founding to today, based on historical information). The Ladino title replaces "Turkish" with "Spanish."

trious Jewish colony negotiated special terms with the city for their burials in a secular cemetery.

Lastly, the Jews of Madrid itself are numerous, and in a certain cemetery—non-Catholic, of course—there is a section reserved for their burials, where you can see their special graves and their headstones in Hebrew letters.

There is, in other words, a foundation on which to build the friendships and literary and mercantile relations you and I desire, which we consider very useful. If men of good faith work together and if the government lends even the most limited assistance, it will not be hard to achieve.

With your talent and erudition, and with the prestige your name carries, you could make the attempt. If so, please count on your affectionate friend as a humble foot soldier in the campaign.

Yours truly,

J. B. Sitges

Chief Customs Officer
January 30, 1904

DAVID ROUSSO[1]

Lawyer in Constantinople, organizer of
Jewish colonies in Palestine

In our third article (page 39), we published a fascinating letter from this respected Jewish lawyer who lives in Constantinople. Here is another. It is, if possible, even more important than the first. Like that first letter, it was written in French. Born in Smyrna in 1875, Mr. Rousso is actively involved in Jewish colonization work in Palestine. The photograph published here, showing him in Bedouin garb, was taken at Tiberias in front of the historic Gate to that city, next to the old fort.

---

[1] Daoud Rousso (1875–unknown): attorney and Zionist organizer. The author admired him greatly and he is one of the correspondents who also appear in Pulido's follow-up book.

Rousso was born in Turkey in the city now known as Izmir. He attended schools run by the Alliance Israélite Universelle, starting with the AIU elementary school in his hometown. As an adult, he served on the AIU Committee in Constantinople, and his enthusiasm for the organization's schools is clear in a speech he gave at an alumni event in 1910.

By 1903, he was legal counsel to the Spanish Embassy in Constantinople and was providing legal advice to the Jewish Colonization Association (JCA), one of the main groups establishing Jewish settlements in the Middle East. A devoted Zionist, he often traveled back and forth between Constantinople and the burgeoning Jewish colonies.

Alti-parmak Han (Constantinople),
February 24, 1904.

HON. MR. PULIDO, SENATOR.

Dear Senator:

I was honored to receive your letter of the 16th. I also received the beautiful issue of La Ilustración Española and your warm letter published in El Liberal [...] I enclose [...] an issue of *Le Monde Illustré*, which, besides a very interesting report on the Jewish farming colonies in Palestine, also contains some notable illustrations.

These colonies are divided into three groups:

1. The Judean group, whose main colonies are Rishon-le-Zion, Petah-Tikvah and Mazkeret-Batya
2. Samaria, whose main colonies are Zichron Yaakov, Atlit, Hedera, Burj and Marah;
3. Galilee, whose main colonies are: Yesod-Hamaalah, Mahanaim, Métouté, Mishmar-Hayarden, Sejera, Abedié, Mesha and Jemma.[2]

The Mikveh Israel agricultural school in Jaffa is a project of the Alliance Israélite, an organization located in Paris. Nearly all the colonies mentioned above belong to the well-

---

[2] *Métouté:* Possibly a mistranscription of Metulah. *Mishmar-Hayarden:* Not to be confused with the modern agricultural community of the same name. *Abedié:* Probably a French phonetic spelling of Bedjen.

DAVID ROUSSO IN BEDOUIN GARB
PHOTOGRAPHED IN TIBERIAS IN FRONT OF
THE HISTORIC GATE, NEXT TO THE OLD FORT

known philanthropist Baron Edmond de Rothschild of Paris. The baron has entrusted the management of his colonies to a fine organization: the Jewish Colonization Association, founded in London by Baron Maurice de Hirsch, with 300 million francs in capital contributed almost entirely by Baron de Hirsch himself. The human race has rarely produced such grand benefactors. The Colonization Association paid taxes to the English government totalling 30 million francs, equal to 10% of Baron de Hirsch's bequest.

The Association has also founded some farming colonies of its own in Palestine. However, its greatest work takes place in Argentina, where it owns numerous large colonies.

I have written to Beirut to ask Mr. S. Y. Pariente,[3] Director General of the Palestinian colonies, to send you photographs. Mr. Pariente occupies a very important position in this matter. Though now a French citizen, he is Spanish by birth and loves Spain dearly. A native of Morocco, he speaks admirable proper Spanish. When he was the Director of the Alliance schools, he made every effort to extend the use of Spanish—true Spanish—among the Jews of the East.

The main newspapers published in Judeo-Spanish in this country (Turkey) are:

- Constantinople: *El Tiempo*, sixteen pages, twice a week. *El Telegrafo*, three times a week.

---

[3] Shemtob Joseph Pariente (1849–1907). Headmaster of half a dozen Alliance schools from the 1870s to 1890s. Director general of the Jewish Colonization Association's Middle Eastern colonies from 1900 to 1905.

- Smyrna: *La Esperanza, Nuvellista* and *Meseret*, all weekly. This last is published in the Turkish language and in Judeo-Spanish.

- Salonika: *El Avenir, La Epoca.*

Among Jews over forty, business correspondence occurs in Judeo-Spanish. Young people prefer French, which they know, and they look down on Judeo-Spanish as a mere jargon.

In Salonika, where Jews make up 60% or more of the population, the Moslems and Christians find they need to learn Spanish.

Feel free to contact me if you need more information.

If you believe I might be of some service to the Royal Academy of the Language in Madrid, I shall be very pleased to accommodate whatever it requests, if it is within my power.

Elías Pasha told me he wrote to you about this a month ago.

I look forward to the honor and pleasure of your reply.

Sincerely yours,

D. Rousso

ENRIQUE BEJARANO

Rabbi and Headmaster of the
Spanish-Jewish School in Bucharest

We have received several letters from the honorable Mr.
Enrique Bejarano, headmaster of the Spanish-Jewish
School in Bucharest. The main letter, dated November
20, 1903, appeared in the first two articles and was of
great help in preparing them. Below are the previously
unused portions of later letters from him.

Bucharest, December 20, 1903.

Dear illustrious sir:

If ever I might envy something, it surely would be those
fortunate people whose rhetorical gifts let them describe
the stirrings of the soul.

Oh, were I like them, my very dear sir, I should use bold
colors and worthy expressions to convey my boundless devotion and deep gratitude for your courteous, gentle attention to a frail, obscure man like me.

The noble wording of your beautiful letters brings tears
of happiness to my eyes.

They cheer my heart and brighten the days of my ad-
vancing years: like a divine angel, sent by God, were you for
me, for my grieving family in particular, and for our entire

race, which feels such affection for people like you who take its well-being to heart.

To answer the question in your most recent letter:

As I said last time, I have not yet been able to publish my literary works on various topics, written in several languages. I lack the means, given the heavy obligations associated with my large family (may God bless them). Still, some of my writings have appeared in European newspapers and magazines such as *L'Univers Israélite* and *Archives Israélites* in Paris; *Boletín de la Enseñanza* in Madrid; *Hamagid* in Lick, Germany; *Ibri* in Brody, Galicia;[1] *Habazeleth* in Jerusalem; *El Correo* and *Dragoman* in Vienna; *El Telegrafo*, *El Instructor* and *El Tiempo* in Constantinople; *El Amigo del Pueblo*, *La Verdad* and *La Alborada* in Bulgaria; and in other newspapers in our country.

All those articles of mine, if collected, surely would make a more or less respectable volume. I also made a translation into elegant Hebrew of the philosophical work "La Religion naturelle" by the late scholar and distinguished philosopher Jules Simon, and a philological explication and annotated edition of the psalms of David, the poet king.[2]

My current project is a collection of some 2,000 proverbs, sayings, legends, tales and folk songs, whose history I

---

[1] *Galicia:* a former Austrian province, now partly in Poland and partly in Ukraine.

[2] **RABBI BEJARANO'S NOTE:** I also have correspondence that I maintained with many non-Jewish scholars, such as the late Jaque Cantacuzine, Prof. Lacroix, the Jorgas, Dr. Oncin, professors and others, about literary matters.

was able to document and explain after much research and study. It includes some expressions and turns of phrase that, at first glance, seem to have lost some of their original meaning, but which make sense if you trace the transformation they underwent over more than four centuries.

This task, as you can imagine, is quite difficult and arduous. It requires rest and time, both of which I sadly lack, given my grueling, exhausting career as a teacher, which weighs on me at this age.

It is only "between light and darkness," as they say here, that I can devote a few moments of leisure to this work, which I find rather interesting. I hope that God will decide to change the circumstances here so that everything will go better!

In reply to your query about contemporary figures noted for their literary knowledge or production:

There are a very respectable number of learned people who, in the East, do fine work in Judeo-Spanish literature and have deep knowledge of it.

However, it is with pride and dignity that we shall mention the distinguished individuals who shine brightest in enriching this literature.

[...]

By today's post, I am sending you an important newspaper from our capital. Its distinguished owner, the eminent lawyer Mr. Mille, is a member of our Parliament's Chamber of Deputies. He was struck by your appeal to the Senate in

Madrid and wrote an article about it. I enclose a translation along with the newspaper.

Incidentally, your speech made a strong impression in our country.[3] As I said, everyone admires your loyal courage and your affection toward my coreligionists.

In fact, my hopes are high!

The results, in all honesty, will be the contentment and happiness of both peoples. I can say unreservedly that if the Spanish government does wish to make an effort to study our race from a literary standpoint, it would profit enormously if it does so with ardent love and without neglect.

I am also sending you some newspapers that I think you will like.

Allow me, my very illustrious friend, to send you an affectionate embrace and say that I remain your very devoted servant,

H. Bejarano
Corbului, 10

P.S.: My dear wife and entire family send respectful greetings to you and your wife and your dear son and daughter. On my own behalf, may all the blessings of Heav-

---

[3] **RABBI BEJARANO'S NOTE:** Our young people are so excited that they are now dying to study Spanish, and would do so if a free course were available. Many have even thought of going abroad to study in Spain. That is how strongly they feel this desire. Believe me, my dear sir: if my commitments allowed me time to teach such a course, I would do them that favor!

en be upon them and favor them. May God keep them well and happy! Amen.

My dear friend, please forgive me if my letter is not pleasing or well written. I am very frail these days, so I am dictating it to my dear daughter and cannot proofread it. I leave it up to you and ask you to do with it as you please.

I hope to God that things will go better for me and that He will be equally caring to you. Your affectionate friend,

Bejarano

————◆————

Bucharest, January 12, 1904

Most illustrious Sir and respected friend Dr. Angel Pulido:

I count myself lucky to have received your lovely previous letter and your informative, humane book, as well as your latest correspondence, dated Jan. 7, and your valiant portrait.

My dear sir, the more time passes, the more you have seen fit to show your affection and friendship to me, your humble servant.

With no exaggeration, I can say that the appearance of your Portrait, that angelic image, has filled my hitherto dark, sorrowful home with light and joy!

Each facial feature bespeaks a virtue, every white hair a wise counsel: that watchful gaze, that paternal affection, that earnest fondness and sweet love for the human race, all shout: Ecce Homo!

Thanks to your prayers for me, I now enjoy perfect health, praised be God, and am continuing my work.

As you requested, I enclose my portrait and I appreciate the use you wish to make of it.

Diamante[4] thought herself the luckiest girl when she read your words of encouragement to her, and especially your noble promise to mail her a small poetry book. She thanks you and kisses your hands.

Please convey my compliments to your Venerable Wife and my affectionate regards to your good, bright children, may God preserve them.

As for you yourself, my Illustrious Sir, your faithful servant prays that God will grant you life and prosperity.

Yours truly,

H. Bejarano

---

[4] **PULIDO'S NOTE:** One of Bejarano's daughters, an elementary school teacher.

Bucharest, February 15, 1904

Most venerable and Illustrious Sir and friend:

I received your beautiful letters and the periodical La Ilustración Española y Americana where I saw my humble portrait well reproduced, for which I am eternally grateful to you.

My dear Sir, if you were here when I was reading your eloquent, wise words from La Ilustración, your tears would doubtless have mingled with mine and those of my wife and children who, around my table, listened to the reading of your letter. It was a missive bearing affection, flowing with paternal friendship for my brothers who were banished from that sweet country, and for my family, who are so taken with you, you illustrious, kind man.

Oh! How it pained my already distressed soul to read your wonderment at my never having visited the motherland: a country that, through the great generosity of men like you, is opening her arms with maternal affection to embrace her children who, without rhyme or reason, were sent away and exiled.

If you, my dear Sir, could read my heart, you would know how it burns with desire to kiss the rocks of that country someday, and bathe my eyes in the dust of the land where my ancestors' bones sleep. I would give robust proof that I am a worthy son of those forebears who transmitted to their children feelings of fidelity and virtue.

That has been my wish since my youth (such patience!!), but as I said, I have not yet been able to afford to go.

I am devastated to read in your last letter that the illustrious Mr. Juan Sitges, the current Chief Customs Officer, who in the past honored me with his dearly appreciated letters, received no reply from me. Oh, never in my life would I do such a thing! I replied as soon as I received his fine card, sending him several books written in Judeo-Spanish, which I now understand he never received.

I take the liberty of enclosing a letter for Mr. Sitges and asking you to forward it to him. Please pardon my boldly inconveniencing you in this way.

As I see it, my literary project will be authoritative. Imagine it, Sir: 2,000 proverbs and sayings explained (most are so concise that they need explaining) will make for a respectable book. If you, a man of judgment, think it appropriate, perhaps we should dedicate[5] it to the Spanish Academy of Languages.

However, I shall do nothing without your advice and counsel, knowing that you serve as a guide and light to me.

I shall say in passing that this project is consuming me, as it requires profound study, serious research and colossal hardship. I am not discouraged, as I find solace in divine protection and the sympathy of good, faithful friends such as you.

These preoccupations revive me and overcome my physical debility; they make me young of heart and spirit. God willing, after Passover I shall start editing my book.

---

[5] *Dedicar* in the original. From context, he may mean 'submit.'

Since you wanted portraits of some of my more prominent brethren, I venture to provide you with pictures of Their Excellencies Elias and Isac Pasha, physicians to His Majesty the Sultan, dressed in formal attire, suitable for publication. Please return them when you are done with them.

My wife and my dear children join me in sending regards to your most venerable wife and your loved ones.

With warm friendship,

Yours truly,

H. Bejarano

Corbului, No. 10

———•———

Bucharest, Feb. 12, 1904

Most Illustrious friend:

Your letter to the students in Vienna, published in *El Liberal*, moved me so deeply that I am sick with affection for your country.

Thousands of thoughts worry my head, to the point where I do not know what world I am in. I feel a deathly nostalgia that saps my soul and eats my heart.

Oh, if only I had wings!! If only I were a dove!..... Yes, my dear Sir, I should be the unhappiest man if I die without seeing the land of my ancestors!

A group of scholars asked me to translate your valuable letter, which I did. Onward! Sir, your enterprise will be engraved on the fabric of our hearts. Every generation will glorify you with praise!

Yours truly,

Bejarano

Regards to your loved ones.

Isaac David Bally[1]

Educator, Secretary/Interpreter of the Board of
Representatives of the Spanish-Jewish Community
of Bucharest, Roumania

Bucharest, February 23, 1904.

To the Hon. Mr. Angel Pulido Martin,[2] Senator.—
Madrid.

Dear Sir:

Thanks to my child's father-in-law, the estimable Mr.
Lazar Ascher, I had the great pleasure of reading your dispatches from Vienna in issues 2603 and 2608 of *Siglo Médi-*

---

[1] Rabbi Isaac David Bally (1842–1922): a noted Jewish educator and
textbook writer in Romania. He was also a translator: his Romanian
Haggadah was used widely in that country.

Of mixed Sephardic and Ashkenazic heritage, he was born into a
well-known banking family. His father, the philanthropist Davicion Bally, was a Jewish community leader who founded multiple charities and
was active in the Haskalah movement. Building on his father's interest in
Jewish education, Rabbi Bally was headmaster of a prestigious Sephardic
school in Bucharest: the Nissim & Lea Halfon Foundation Spanish-Rite
Jewish Community Primary School for Girls (Şcoala Primară de Fete a
Comunităţii Israelite de Rit Spaniol „Fundaţia Nissim şi Lea Halfon").

Some sources spell his first name Isac.

[2] Ángel Pulido Martín was the author's son, whose letters sometimes
appeared in the medical journal *El Siglo Médico*. Here, Rabbi Bally thinks
the father and son are the same person.

co.[3] I found it truly comforting to experience again the growing number of respected men who acknowledge the injustice committed 412 years ago against the ancestors of today's Jews, who, like the captives in Babylon, still cry out, "If I forget thee, O sweet, beloved Spain, let my right hand forget her cunning; let my tongue cleave to the roof of my mouth, if I remember thee not, if I set thee not above my chiefest joy."[4]

Your question to the Minister of State and his favorable response to your exhortation encouraged me to write you these few lines, which might be useful in your noble, generous attempt to right a wrong. That injustice was excusable in a time of universal blindness and ignorance. Its correction can serve Spain's worthy economic and intellectual interests and, in our era, increase and strengthen Spain's role in promoting harmony among the civilized nations of Europe and the Americas.

After this short introduction, let me give my humble view on how best to pursue what you proposed in that appeal.

The first step would be an official repeal of the disastrous edict of 1492.[5] This would, as a result, open the country to any descendants of the Jews expelled in 1492 who

---

[3] **PULIDO'S NOTE:** My son's published letters about his courses and travels.

[4] A variation on Psalm 137, replacing "Jerusalem" with "Spain." The English here is based on the 1917 JPS *Holy Scriptures.*

[5] **PULIDO'S NOTE:** Articles 2 and 11 of the Spanish Constitution already repealed the edict.

wish to regain Spanish citizenship. Spain could issue citizenship papers to all of them through special consuls appointed in each city, chosen mainly from among the descendants of the banished Jews. This would be sufficient to give Spain roughly a million extremely devoted, loyal offspring[6] who are now spread throughout the East.

Some would move to Spain but continue trading with the Jews who stay in their current locales, causing Spanish business and industry to flourish anew and letting Spain's language and literature recover their well-deserved influence.

I enclose a copy of a letter I received seven years ago from Mr. G. Cavadia, the Spanish Consul in Braila,[7] followed by the information that I was asked for in 1897.

If it is not too much trouble, I wonder if you might send me a catalog of the volumes published to date in the series of very affordable books issued by *El Siglo Médico*, along with a sample volume from that series. I would also appreciate the name of a good bookseller from which to occasionally order and obtain books and periodicals from Spain.

Thank you again for your generous intervention on behalf of my coreligionists.

---

[6] **PULIDO'S NOTE:** Mr. Bally's figure of one million may be the most accurate, if we include all the Spanish Jews in Europe, Asia, Africa and the Americas.

[7] George Cavadia (1858–1926): a composer and singer who, starting in the early 1890s, served as Spain's temporary consul in Braila. The book omits Cavadia's letter to Rabbi Bally but reproduces the rabbi's reply.

With affectionate esteem, I remain at your disposal for the advancement of your noble efforts to promote what is good, true and beautiful.

Yours truly,

I. D. Bally

————•————

(Mr. Bally's reply to Mr. Cavadia:)

Bucharest 3 - June 15, 1897.

Dear sir:

In his letter of June 4, 1897, Mr. Jose Reischer of Braila asks me to answer a set of questions that you had posed.

This letter is my reply to your request.

1. Approximately how many Spanish-speaking Jews are there in Bucharest?

A. 320 families or 1600 souls (320 x 5 = 1600)

2. How is the Spanish Jewish Community organized?

A. For worship, they have two synagogues:[8]

---

[8] Bucharest's two Sephardic synagogues were the Great Spanish Temple (Kahal Kadosh Gadol, built in the 1810s) and the nearby Small Spanish Temple on the Strada Spaniolă (Kahal Kadosh Shalom, built in the 1840s to address a rift between religious traditionalists and a reform-

The first, called *Kahal Kadosh Gadol,* at 10 Negru Voda Street, with 314 seats for men and 146 for women, has an *annual budget* of 22,000 *francs,* and a choir and organ. They use the organ only for weddings and on the three most important holidays of the Mosaic calendar;

The second, called *Kahal Kadosh Shalom,* with 150 seats for men and 70 for women, has a *budget* of 6,000 *francs per year.* This synagogue is on a street whose name translates as *Spanish Street.*

Each synagogue is administered by a five-man committee. The Kahal Kadosh Gadol Committee consists of Messrs. Moise N. Halfon, Haim Russo, Lazar Ascher, I. Moisescu and Mosen Iacob Termo. The Kahal Kadosh Shalom Committee comprises Messrs. Isac Josef Termo, M. E. Cohen, M. D. Algazy, Efrayim Nahmias and David Solomon.

3. A Council of seven Representatives serves as the Community's board. The Committees that administer our Community institutions report to the board.

4. The President of our Community is the highly esteemed and beloved Mr. Solomon Josef Halfon.

---

ist faction). The Great Temple was remodeled and enlarged in the 1850s and again in the 1880s and 90s. In this last renovation, the architect Grigore Cerchez used Spanish and Moorish motifs, evoking the decor of old synagogues in Spain.

Both temples survived until the Holocaust, when the Iron Guard riot of 1941 destroyed twenty-five Bucharest synagogues and left more than 120 Jews dead.

5. The names of the other Representatives and of members of the various Committees appear in the 1896 report, which you will receive by mail with this letter.

The report and the attached bylaws will give you any details you may wish to know about our community.

6. The Representatives and the members of the various Committees enjoy solid social standing and are well regarded by their fellow Jews and by the Christians of Bucharest.

7. Commercial importance: Except for a few affluent banking firms known throughout Europe and some 500 souls reduced to accepting aid from their brothers, the rest earn a middling income making goods or working on commission. There are some doctors, teachers, architects, engineers, artisans, typographers and lithographers, but very few people work in industry.

8. Education: Every boy completes 4 years of primary school and many go on to secondary schools, commercial schools or even universities.

The same can be said of the girls.

9. In Bucharest there is not even one periodical in the Judeo-Spanish language.

10. Until 30 years ago, businessmen and all other Spanish Jews wrote to each other and did their bookkeeping in

the Judeo-Spanish language, written in the Hebrew alphabet. Today, they and their families mainly use Roumanian. Despite this, the Spanish dialect continues to be spoken in nearly every Spanish-Jewish home in Bucharest. All families, however, without exception, also use Roumanian.

11. In our community's Jewish schools, students translate Bible texts into both Judeo-Spanish and Roumanian.

12. The Spanish Jews are more respected by the Christian population. If not for the numerous Polish Jews in Roumania, the Spanish Jews would have been emancipated long ago.

13. In Roumania there are still Spanish communities in these cities: Craiova, Turnu Severin, Calafat, Corabia, Ploiesti, Giurgiu[9] and Kalarash.
The structure of these Communities is almost the same as in the capital.

14. In these seven communities, there are approximately: Craiova 100 families = 500 souls, Turnu Severin 40 families = 200 souls, Calafat and Corabia 20 families = 100 souls, Ploieşti 40 families = 200 souls, Giurgiu 50 families = 250 souls and, lastly, Kalarash with 40 families = 200 souls; Constanta with 30 families = 150 souls.

---

[9] "Giusgiu" in the original book; almost certainly a typographical error.

In the province of *Muntenia*, there are still a few towns with no more than 2 or 3 Spanish-Jewish families or even just one individual.

This is, in short, the response I can offer to your questions. To conclude, dear sir, it will always be my pleasure to be at the prompt service of the esteemed representative of the always beloved and sweet Spain.

I. D. Bally.

————•————

Bucharest - March 11, 1904.

TO THE HON. MR. ANGEL PULIDO MARTIN, Senator. Madrid.

Dear Sir:

To avoid further delay in answering your kind letter of March 2, 1904, I am writing this short note today. When I receive the catalog and sample volume from the discount library collection, I shall write to confirm receipt.

I am well aware that the Spanish Constitution repeals all laws, decrees, etc., that violate its guarantees of tolerance. Even so, an edict expressly repealing the 1492 decree is vital. With such an edict, the Spanish government would perform an act of the utmost justice, publicly stressing that the repeal acknowledges the cruel injustice and iniquity committed against a completely blameless population, and that it is granting full Spanish citizenship to any descendants of the ill-fated victims of the 1492 edict who express a desire to become Spaniards again, whether they stay where they are or resume residency in Spain.

This government edict would build on the great strides the Spanish nation already took with the rogations held at every church in Spain in 1857 at the urging of Mr. Luis Amador de los Rios. A new edict revoking the 1492 decree, printed in thousands of copies posted and proclaimed in every Jewish temple around the world, would have a prompt, salubrious effect. It will bring Spain thousands of good, faithful progeny, now lost but always ready to reignite the country's finances and give new flight to their dear mother's industry, trade and civilizing power. This would verify the words of the above-mentioned public rogation of 1857, which ended with these sweet, consoling words:

"And if Thou, O God of Abraham, wilt bring back Thy children to Spain, we shall not forget Thy promise: 'I shall bless them that bless thee.'"

I can recommend the following good booksellers:

- Libraria Generala, run by Emil Storck (which I use for my own needs),

- The Libraria Universala of Leon Alcalay (a Spanish Jew), and finally

- Messrs. Soceck & Co., booksellers.

All three are on *Calea Victoriei* (Victory Street), and are well known within and beyond Roumania.

Once again, I remain at your service and that of the Spanish government.

Regards from your devoted and faithful servant.

I. D. Bally

Lázaro Ascher[1]

Distinguished business owner, banker, defender of Jewish culture. We already published two short letters of his in article III (page 35). The longer letter below contains curious facts and some personal information that we urged him to include. We apologize to the illustrious Mr. Ascher for making this public, but we consider it a valuable informational document.

---

[1] Lazar Ascher (1839–unknown): businessman and community leader. Born to an affluent textile-importing family, Ascher grew up in Bucharest and studied business in Dresden. He was active in many Jewish community projects led by his elder brother, the philanthropist Moscu Ascher (1826/27–1905).

The brother, Moscu, first gained attention as a Jewish educational reformer in mid-nineteenth-century Bucharest, and went on to develop scholarships and vocational training programs for Jewish youth. Moscu was a board member of organizations such as Bucharest's Sephardic Community Council, the Romanian committee of the Alliance Israélite Universelle, the Sinai philanthropic society, and the Zionist organization Choweve Sion. His strongest ties, however, were to the boys' school run by Rabbi Bejarano, which he visited almost daily. As a young man, Moscu had married into the wealthy Halfon family. For many years, the Halfons provided most of the operating money for the city's two private Sephardic schools.

By the late 1870s, Lazar and Moscu were both on the board of the Bucharest Sephardic Jewish Primary Schools Society (a.k.a. the Talmud Torah Committee). They served on its board for more than twenty years. A roster from 1900 shows Moscu as president and Lazar as vice president. After Moscu's death, Lazar assumed the presidency. He was still on the board as late as 1910, as vice president. Lazar was also active in the Great Spanish Temple of Bucharest: he was, for instance, the contact person when the synagogue advertised for a new cantor in 1900.

Bucharest, February 16, 1904.

Esteemed sir and dear friend:

It was an indescribable pleasure to receive your fine letter of the 29th of last month, together with the two issues of "El Siglo Médico." I also enjoyed reading the praiseworthy description of your trip and what you saw in our city (incidentally, for "city," we say *ciodad* instead of *ciudad*), for which I thank you very much. I was equally overjoyed to learn you are writing articles about the Spanish Jews, and that you want me to send photographs of our Temple and School. I am glad to say I acted quickly (we say *en lugo*, not *en luego*) and had photos taken of two parts of the Temple's Moorish-style interior and of the facade. I also had photos taken of our Jewish Community Schools for boys and for girls. I hope these are of use to you. I beg (*rogo* here, not *ruego*) your forgiveness for the delay, but it took some testing to be sure the pictures came out perfectly and I only just got them back today. One was taken facing the Altar: at right you will recognize our friend Mr. E. Bejarano in priestly robes, as he is also our Temple's Preacher, and at left is Mr. David Isac, the Temple's main Minister and officiating Cantor. The second picture shows the other end of the Temple, including the main entrance and, above that, the choir loft and organ. The other three photos show the facades of the Temple, the Boys' School, and the Girls' School.

I am sending you prints of these five photographs, which I think will meet your needs.

MR. LÁZARO ASCHER
PRESIDENT OF THE BOARD OF THE SYNAGOGUE
AND OF THE SPANISH-JEWISH SCHOOLS OF BUCHAREST

The Temple, built (we say *fraguado*) in 1817 and rebuilt in 1852, has 350 seats for men downstairs and 150 for women up in the gallery. The left and right galleries have entrances separate from the entry to the lower level. Our Community has had its Boys' School since 1730. The school did not originally have its own space, but in 1817 four rooms (we say *camaretas*) were built for it on the grounds (*cortijo*) of the synagogue, and in 1894 the current building was erected. It is overseen by a five-man Committee. The Institute bears the name "School for Sons of the Spanish Israelite Community."

The narrow street to the left (we say *izquiedra*), which is the Temple's alleyway (*calleja*), is called "Strada Spaniola."

Our Community has had its Girls' School since 1878. The sons and sons-in-law of the late Nissim and Lea Halfon donated 60,000 francs through their foundation, and the School is called the "Nissim & Lea Halfon Foundation School for Daughters of the Spanish Israelite Community." The education is the same as at the Boys' School. It teaches the national curriculum in Roumanian, and Religion and the Bible in Spanish. Primary education lasts four years. The current building was erected in 1891 at a cost of 120,000 francs. The five-man Committee is the same as for the Boys' School, but this Institution also has a Ladies' Committee consisting of Mrs. Esther S. Halfon, wife of the President of our Community, Mr. Salomon J. Halfon; Mrs. Sarah S. Rizo, a co-founder of this Institute, daughter of the late Nissim and Lea Halfon; and Mrs. Thamara L. Ascher, my wife. This is a permanent Committee with lifetime appointments that the foundation made in 1878. My brother and his wife,

MRS. THAMARA ASCHER
WIFE OF MR. L. ASCHER

Paloma, a daughter of the late N. & L.H., are no longer living. I am anxious to hear from you that the photographs are publishable. Despite my best efforts, we could do no better in the winter light.

After all these centuries, the Spanish Jews preserve a striking number of old customs. For instance, we refer to parents, older siblings and aged relatives as *Señor Padre*, *Señora Madre* and so on. We address them with the formal "you" (not *tú*), and on holidays we kiss their hands. We address old men and old women who are not our relatives as *Tío* (Uncle) or *Tía* (Aunt). If a child falls down, people say to him "la hora buena" ("I wish you well") or "crescas como el piscadico en agua fresca" ("may you grow like a little fish in fresh water"). When a child sneezes, they say "crescas y enflorescas" ("may you grow and flourish"). Even meals differ from those of our neighbors and closely resemble those of Spanish Jews in other places. For instance, they cook Almodrote (eggplant, with fat or oil, with cheese), Cucharicas (made by cutting an eggplant in two, scalding it, scooping out the inside and mixing this with egg and cheese, chopping the mixture with a wooden knife to keep it from turning black, stuffing it back into the skins and frying them in fat or olive oil). They also eat lentils on Fridays, which I imagine was an old Spanish custom because the great Cervantes says Don Quixote ate lentils on Fridays. Meatballs.

They bake treats with Spanish names such as pastellilos, pastel, bollos (even on the street, you hear people shout "Bollicos!"), quesadas, roscas (made with dough, flour, oil

SPANISH-JEWISH TEMPLE
THE COMMUNITY'S TEMPLE IN BUCHAREST

and egg) filled with alhasuo[2] (a finely crushed mixture of nuts and crunchy cookies, with honey), marzipan, musta-chudo (made with a small amount of flour, with sugar and wet almonds), and almendrada. Clearly I am no cook, so forgive the talk of food, but I wanted to show again how much my fellow Jews preserve your language and customs. Even our fellow Bucharesters call us simply "Spanioli," Spaniards, as if we were members of the noble Spanish nation (if only that had been God's will).

Now let me tell you a bit about my family.[3] My Father was born here in 1797 and my Mother in 1804. In 1813, my Father inherited my Grandfather's business, selling English fabric imported via Constantinople. My father was the first to import directly from England: cotton, thread and tools, filling entire ships. I was born in 1839, on March 8, and I learned Roumanian, French and German. In 1857 my Father sent me to Dresden, where I graduated from the School of Business, and in 1860 I joined my Father's business. My three older brothers already held responsible positions in the firm, and my Father gave me stock and I became a partner. In 1861 I began traveling to Austria, Germany, France, England, Switzerland, Belgium, Holland and Italy three times a year, so I would be here for a month and then away on business for three months. In 1863 my Father retired and

---

[2] *Alhasuo*: from the Ibero-Arabic *al-hasú* ('the filling'). In Jewish cuisine today, the word survives in the name of traditional Sephardic Purim cookies: *roscas di alhasu* (literally 'ring-shaped baked items with filling'). In modern Spanish, *al-hasú* evolved into *alfajor* ('filled cookie').

[3] **PULIDO'S NOTE:** At our request.

INTERIOR OF THE SPANISH SYNAGOGUE
OF BUCHAREST
(FACING THE ALTAR)

left his four sons to carry on the company. In 1866 we lost my Mother and a year later my Father, may they rest in peace.

My Father left four identical wills, one for each son, written in Spanish in the Hebrew alphabet. The advice it contained included this: "You know, my dear ones, that our family's watchword is 'Honor before earnings.' That was a legacy from my Father, your Grandfather, and now I leave it to you. I followed it most religiously. May you do the same, and so may the children of your children forever." All of us did follow it, and still guard it like the eyes in our heads.

In 1873 two of my brothers left the business. One went to Vienna and the other to Paris. In 1876 my older brother and I established a bank here, the Bank of Bucharest, with ten million francs in capital, along with eight other founders, including Princes Démètre Ghica and Alex. Styrbey. After six years, we liquidated the Bank. It had not been right for us—though it was still giving us 17 to 18% dividends a year—because every day either my brother or I had to go to Board meetings or senior management meetings, and all the founders were neglecting our own businesses, and my brothers are now dead. I left the business 14 years ago.

In 1872 I married a daughter of the late Lázaro de Mayo. The languages I know are Spanish (as you can tell), Roumanian, French, Italian, German, English. I also have a reading knowledge of Hebrew.

My wife knows Spanish, Roumanian, French, German and English, and plays the piano. I have three children. The

INTERIOR OF THE SPANISH SYNAGOGUE
OF BUCHAREST
(FACING THE ORGAN)

eldest son, now 24, graduated from the local lyceum with great success and earned his diploma, and also graduated from the conservatory here, winning the top prize. Now he is at the University of Liege, where he passed every exam with distinction, the last of which granted him the title of Candidat Ingénieur avec distinction (Engineering Candidate with Distinction). He knows Spanish, Roumanian, French, German and English, belongs to two music appreciation societies, and is much loved by all who know him, including some Spaniards he knows there named Moreno, who mistook him for a fellow Spaniard. Our second child is our 18-year-old daughter, Lucia, named after my mother, who has the honor of maintaining correspondence with your dear daughter. Our friend Mr. E. Bejarano tells me they resemble each other greatly. She knows Spanish, French, German and Roumanian, plays the piano and paints.

The third is León, aged 13. After completing all four primary-school years at our Spanish School, he is now in his second year at the local Business School. He knows Spanish, Roumanian, French and German, and plays the piano. During my frequent travels, my greatest pleasure was to make the acquaintance of Spaniards in the hotel where I was staying and spend the evening with them. It was almost like being at home.

One night in 1878, when I was in Paris with a Jewish friend from here, we were coming back from the Opera House with a Spanish gentleman whose name escapes me. As we entered the hotel and were talking of Spain, we thought of possibly traveling there. Our Spanish companion was to return there two days later, and we considered taking advantage of the timing. The three of us spent the night with an atlas and timetables, trying to figure out whether it was practical in the few days we had. But business comes before pleasure, and we needed to be at a trade show in Leipzig. So we gave up the trip to the land where orange trees blossom.[4] And since he who hesitates is lost, I missed my chance to see the land of my ancestors, which we all hold so dear.

Just now, as I was about to end this letter, I received La Ilustración Española. Thank you a thousand times over. I read it to my family and we were overcome with pleasure and delight at all your efforts and your praiseworthy patriotism.

God speed your work. I remain at your disposal.

Sincerely,

Lazaro Ascher.

---

[4] Given Ascher's knowledge of German, this may be a paraphrased reference to the Goethe novel *Wilhelm Meister's Apprenticeship*. In that book, the character of Mignon sings a song of longing for her native Italy, which begins "Do you know the land where the lemon trees blossom...?" ("Kennst du das Land, wo die Zitronen blühn...?").

MR. LÁZARO ASCHER
AS A YOUNG MAN

Bucharest, February 24, 1904.

Esteemed sir and dear friend:

I take the liberty of enclosing a Spanish translation of a poem composed in Hebrew by the distinguished poet Abulhassan Yehuda Ben-Samuel Halevi, known as Judah Halevy, born in old Castile in 1086.[5] Like all verse by this great poet, philosopher and physician, who was much sought after in Toledo, this text is sung in all Spanish-Jewish temples in all countries, always in Spanish and, curiously, always with the same melodies, reflecting their origin in Spain.

Our prayer books contain all the poems by this sage and by others born in Spain, translated into Spanish in Hebrew letters. However, I copied this poem from a small daily prayer book inherited from my father, God rest his soul, who inherited it from my ancestors. It is only in Spanish (with no Hebrew) and was printed in the year 5494 (our year counting from the creation of the world), 1734, and is paraphrased from the Book of Esther. This poem is sung in the Temple in Spanish by five students from our School on the Sabbath before the holiday of "Purim." This year, it is this coming Sabbath, February 27, and the holiday of Purim falls on Tuesday, March 1.

You no doubt had heard of the poet Judah Halevy, who wrote poems not only in Hebrew but also in Arabic and Spanish. To our misfortune, we have only his Hebrew verse.

---

[5] **PULIDO'S NOTE:** Not included in this volume.

His poems in other languages were burned and lost. If we had them today, Spain would be so honored to have possessed such great geniuses eight centuries ago. I also take the liberty of enclosing a poem by the poet Heinrich Heine, entitled "Jehuda Halevi," with which you are surely familiar, in which he praises this erudite gentleman.

Thank you for sending the newspaper "El Liberal," in which I was happy to read your letter to the president of the organization La Esperanza in Vienna. Let me say (just between us) you were right to call the Spanish of the Viennese Jews an error-laden jargon.[6] If they speak a ten-word sentence, four words are in degenerated Spanish and the other six are German with an Austrian dialect. This is because their schools do not teach Religion and the Bible in Spanish, and their prayer books include German translations (even the ones we have with Spanish translations come from Vienna) and not pure Spanish transcribed into Hebrew letters. They do not speak this beautiful language at home and do not give sermons at Temple in this language. While they have and do everything in German, we have and do everything in Spanish, as Jews do in the East. Last Sabbath, our friend Mr. Bejarano gave such a beautiful sermon in Spanish in the Temple. In Vienna they cannot do this, as we do here and in the East, because their younger generations will not understand or comprehend it, which is why I allow my-

---

[6] It was the Vienna student organization La Esperanza, not Pulido, that described Ladino as an "error-laden jargon." Pulido merely quoted them.

self to hope that all your efforts to propagate Spanish will be crowned with success.

With deepest respect.

Sincerely,

Lázaro Ascher.

M. GAÑY[1]

Head of an agency representing the Nationala
insurance companies in Rosiori, Roumania

In article III (page 34) we published another of his
letters.

In article III (page 34)

Rosiori, Feb. 26, 1904.

Dear Mr. Pulido:

Your beautiful letter of the 11th arrived promptly and it
is my pleasure to reply.

We are so happy that honorable men of position in our
Mother Country are taking an interest in the Spanish Jews.

Establishing affectionate relations between Spain and
her children in the East will take a lot of effort: I believe the
Spanish have forgotten their far-off brothers and that the
Hebrews have lost hope of ever seeing their Motherland.

---

[1] M. Gani (fl. 1890s–1910s): co-owner of the Gheorghiu & Gani insur-
ance agency in Rosiori, Romania; a former student of Rabbi Bejarano's.
Additional correspondence from this affluent entrepreneur appears in
Pulido's follow-up book.

As previously noted, Gani's Ladino is strikingly different from modern Spanish. There are archaisms, unusual transcriptions into the Latin
alphabet, and a strong influence of French and Italian. When unsure of a
word, he adds a French translation in parentheses: "coraçon (coeur),"
"aspero (j'attende)." In one case, he simply puts the French "introduire"
in quotation marks, followed by an explanation that mixes Italian and
Spanish elements: "non conosco la palabra" ("I do not know the word").

The movement you are undertaking with your articles in Spanish periodicals, which are read by Jews in the East, awakens in us a feeling that lay hidden at the bottom of our heart.

Yes, we speak Spanish and always call ourselves "Spanish Jews," and our communities are separate from those of other Jews. We do not mix at all with the people known as German Jews.[2]

We retain a Spaniard's fine, proud character and are proud of our origin.

What happened four centuries ago is forgotten, and if the Grandees of Spain see fit, Spain will become involved in schools in the East to "introduire" (I do not know the word) the Spanish language into the classrooms.

Clearly this will entail some sacrifice on Spain's part, but many thousands of hearts will think of their dear Motherland with much more love and interest. The language we speak is surely mixed with many foreign words, and we cannot express ourselves as sweetly as we should like. Those of us who had some schooling in Spanish literature are far behind the times.

It was a great pleasure to read the periodicals I received, and their sweet articles inspired in me a feeling of recognition.

I sent the periodicals to my friends. Could you please subscribe me to "El Liberal"? I shall send you the cost of a six-month subscription.

---

[2] *The people known as German Jews:* Ashkenazic Jews. Jewish documents from Romania in this era usually refer to Ashkenazim as "Western-Rite Jews" and Sephardim as "Spanish-Rite" or "Eastern-Rite Jews."

MR. M. GAÑY
HEAD OF A LARGE AGENCY IN ROSIORI, ROUMANIA

Rosiori, Feb. 26, 1904.

To Mr. Pulido.

I sent my teacher, Mr. Bejarano, an issue of El Liberal, which I think he will enjoy very much.

I await the promised dictionary and wonder if you could please also enclose two or three books of advice on the Spanish language. I shall reimburse you for all of these.

Thank you in advance. Also, please let me know if you can understand everything I write.

I get the impression my style is hard to understand, as not all the words are in modern Spanish.

Warm regards and a friendly handshake.

M. Gañy.

Moises Fresco[1]

Distinguished educator, headmaster of the Jewish boys'
school that the Alliance Israélite Universelle founded in
Galata, author of several education books,
Judeo-Spanish journalist

Constantinople, February 10, 1904.

Mr. A. Pulido, Senator—Madrid.

Sir:

I was fascinated and most happy to read the words you
spoke in the Senate on November 13. I am writing this letter
of thanks in the Judeo-Spanish language that we use here,
except that we write it in rabbinical characters.

---

[1] Moïse Fresco (1859–1912): teacher and headmaster at various AIU
schools in Turkey from the 1880s to 1909. His published works include
teachers' manuals and numerous textbooks for elementary and secondary schools. In 1889, Sultan Abdul Hamid II decorated him with the Order of the Medjidie.

Pulido calls him a journalist but, as Fresco points out in his letter of
February 24, 1904, the author confused him with the newspaper editor
David Fresco. Moïse Fresco did, however, publish a twice-weekly bilingual magazine for teachers from 1889 to 1891 in Smyrna: *El Maestro*
(איל מאאיסטרו, also known by its Turkish title, *Oustad*). He left the AIU
schools in 1909 to work for the Turkish Ministry of Public Education and
to join the faculty of the Constantinople Teachers' College.

Not to be confused with Rabbi Moïse Fresco (1780–1850), who had
been the chief rabbi of Constantinople.

Surely you will understand me, since we did not need a dictionary to understand the transcript you thoughtfully sent to Mr. Dalmedigo. After sharing it with several fellow Jews in Constantinople, I translated it into French and sent it to Paris, to French friends who do not know Spanish.

You were right about the warm feelings we Eastern Jews all profess for the Spanish language. Even as a child, I was curious to read something in Spanish, but I could never find a book in this language.

The first time I was able to find a text in this beautiful tongue was in a French book, Corneille's *Le Cid*, which also included the ballads about El Cid:

> Delante el rey de León
> Doña Ximena una tarde
> Se pone á pedir justicia
> Por la muerte de su padre, etc.

> Before the king of León
> One afternoon Doña Ximena
> Begins to petition for justice
> For the death of her father, etc.

I was amazed to find I understood it all, as if it were in our own native language, which it is.

When I spent time in Tangier, Morocco (twenty years ago), I had the chance to read some works in Spanish, especially *Don Quixote* by Cervantes, which impressed me greatly. That was the moment when I really understood the huge

M. FRESCO
JOURNALIST, HEADMASTER OF THE
ALLIANCE ISRAÉLITE SCHOOL FOR BOYS
IN GALATA, CONSTANTINOPLE

difference between a translation and its original. I had enjoyed Don Quixote's adventures in a French translation, but I still did not see why it deserved universal acclaim or should be called a masterpiece. However, reading the original, I understood and knew it was worthy of all the praise and enthusiasm it inspires, for I felt the enthusiasm myself. I realized that the best thing about this book is not the adventures, as entertaining as they are, but the naturalness and truth of the characters and speech. The dialogue is full of Don Quixote's wit and judgments and Sancho's delicious words, which even the best translation cannot capture.

"Traduttore, traditore" say the Italians, and (if memory serves) Cervantes' hero compares an original work and its translation to a tapestry: the original is the front and the translation the back. A very apt comparison.

Reading the book, I also felt a kind of echo in my heart and seemed to hear a familiar, beloved voice: though the characters were from a distant time, they reminded me of my contemporaries and my family. For instance, when Juana was talking and complaining to Sancho, I could almost hear one of our lower-class Jewish women from Haskeuy or Balat (in Constantinople). Everything in this superior book is sweet, funny and pleasant.

I have also read other Spanish books, and one I liked very much was *The Seagull* by Fernán Caballero. I especially enjoyed the part where old María and Brother Gabriel care for a sick stranger. "Perhaps he is a Jew," says Brother Gabriel. "God help us!" the old woman cries. "But stay! If he were a Jew, shouldn't we have seen his tail when we undressed him?"[2]

This novel includes a song very similar to some folk songs sung by our old women in Turkey.

Here are the first four lines:

> Estando un caballerito
> en la isla de León
> se enamoró de una dama,
> y ella le correspondió.

> When a young cavalier
> Was on the isle of León
> He fell in love with a lady,
> Who requited his love.

Spanish theater, so original and so little known around the world, has provided me with good reading. I enjoyed plays such as *Guzmán the Good* (by Gil y Zárate, I think), which is so dramatic. Also *Die and You'll See* (by Bretón): I wonder why there is no French translation of this comedy (*dont la donnée est extremement originale*).[3]

---

[2] **FRESCO'S NOTE:** I copied down several pages of this novel, which paints such a vivid portrait of folk customs and ideas in Andalusia.

TRANSLATOR'S NOTE: Dialogue is quoted here from Augusta Bethell's English translation, *The Sea-gull*, published in London by Richard Bentley in 1867. That edition omits the song, which I have translated literally.

[3] French for "...whose premise is extremely original."

I also read Cadolso's Moroccan letters, which resemble Montesquieu's *Lettres persanes*, and the excellent translation of *Gil Blas*. But this was all twenty years ago.

I am happy that this opportunity arose to recall these excellent works of which I have fond memories.

With esteem and regards.

M. Fresco

———•———

Constantinople, February 10, 1904.

Sir:

I am sorry to have missed you when you were in our city. I would be very glad to receive a picture of you. If I had one of myself, I would have mailed it to you. However, I enclose a portrait of my son and daughter.

I also enclose a copy of the holy story, part 1 (from the creation to the death of Moses), written in Judeo-Spanish in rabbinical Hebrew characters, which I composed and published for our little students in the small Jewish schools known as *Talmud-Torahs*.

Yours truly,

M. Fresco.

MOISÉS FRESCO'S CHILDREN
CONSTANTINOPLE

Constantinople, February 12, 1904.

Mr. Pulido—Madrid.

Dear Sir:

This is further to my letter of the 10th and the copy of the holy story written in Judeo-Spanish, aimed at young students in our primary schools. In that booklet, I took pains not to mix in any words from Turkish, Hebrew, Italian or French, and to come as close as possible to Castilian Spanish while remaining understandable to most of the children.

You may be curious to see some lines from this booklet transcribed into Latin characters. Here are the second and third paragraphs of the first page:

> *Creation of man.* And God said, "Let us make man in our shape and likeness, and give him domain over all the animals." And God formed man's body from the dust of the earth and gave him the spirit of life and called him Adam. After completing all these works, God rested on the seventh day and sanctified it.

> *Garden of Eden.* God placed Adam in a beautiful garden called the "Garden of Eden." In this garden one could find[4] all manner of trees pleasant to the eye and pleasing

---

[4] **FRESCO'S NOTE:** *Topar,* meaning 'to find,' is old Spanish. I have encountered this verb in *Don Quixote.* In *Don Quixote* I also found the word *desmasalado*, meaning 'unfortunate.' *Desmasalado* comes from the Hebrew *mazal* (מזל in Hebrew characters).

to the taste. In the middle of the garden stood the tree of the knowledge of good and evil...

Yours truly,

M. Fresco.

I have also translated and published in Spanish, as close as possible to Castilian Spanish, the report of the general meeting of the Alliance Israélite held in Paris on April 29, 1903.

———— • ————

Constantinople, Feb. 24, 1904.

Dear Sir:

A thousand thanks for your kind letter, which has given me such great pleasure. Though we retain the old language of Spain, we were unable to preserve the type of fluent expression and exquisite terms in which I should like to express my appreciation. Our language is very poor in these expressions. Let me just say I shall keep your letter among my prized mementos and souvenirs. There was some confusion about names in your letter. My name is Moises Fresco and I am, as I had the honor to tell you, headmaster of the Alliance school in Galata. Mr. David Fresco, who is my friend, edits the newspaper "El Tiempo." Both of us fight against ignorance, though in different spheres. My experience as an author is limited to school textbooks and teachers' guides, written mainly in French.

To render unto Caesar that which is Caesar's, as soon as I received your beautiful letter, I went to the offices of El Tiempo and read Mr. Fresco the portion addressed to and regarding him, and he was very moved by your praise.

I have read with great interest your magnificent letter in El Liberal addressed to the young Jews of Vienna. Those sweet words and that simple, impassioned eloquence went straight to my heart and I trust they will be fruitful. The article will make a strong impression on all who read it. I have sent one of the two copies of the newspaper to Mr. Jacques Danon of Adrianople (not to be confused with Abraham Danon, head of the rabbinical seminary of Constantinople). Last year, Mr. Jacques Danon mounted a campaign in favor of the lovely Spanish language in the newspaper "La Epoca" in Salonika. He published a series of articles in that paper asking people to stop using Judeo-Spanish over time and start writing in the Latin alphabet, and he even developed plans to found a newspaper here in pure Spanish printed in Latin characters. He did not have time to execute that project and therefore asked for my cooperation and participation.

I should be honored to read anything you may care to write to me.

Your affectionate servant,

M. Fresco.

P.S. Mr. David Ruso informed me that since you had asked him for portraits, he has sent you a photograph of me that was in his possession.

———•———

Constantinople, March 2, 1904.

Mr. A. Pulido.

My dear sir:

I received the issue of "El Liberal" in which you published my letter. I am happy that it appeared in print because it has garnered me very warm letters and good wishes from various parts of Spain; and this is a source of great pleasure and happiness for me and my family and friends.

Mr. Cansino Assens[5] of Madrid wrote me a very affectionate letter, so complimentary I cannot bring myself to quote it to you; my letter you published does not deserve

---

[5] Rafael Cansinos Assens (1882–1964): prolific Spanish author, critic and translator.

As a boy, he learned that his father was descended from *conversos* (Jews who converted to Catholicism to avoid expulsion). Cansinos Assens developed an abiding interest in Judaism and embraced Jewish identity during much of his adult life, though he does not appear to have formally converted. His Jewish-themed writings include the books *España y los judíos españoles* (Spain and the Spanish Jews, 1920), *Los judíos en la literatura española* (The Jews in Spanish literature, 1937) and *Los judíos en Sefarad* (The Jews in Sepharad, 1950).

such praise. Mr. Assens tells me he would be pleased to send me articles for publication in newspapers here. Enclosed you will find a copy of my reply to Mr. Assens. In that response, you will see why at present it is not practical for our Spanish-language press to use anything other than Hebrew characters, despite what you and I would prefer. We have considered this question on several occasions. Before any other steps, we need to educate a new generation and gradually accustom them to this reform, and the change should involve more than switching alphabets. We must also move closer to pure Spanish, which only a few journalists use: most of our editors write a jargon mixed heavily with other languages. To dress "jargon" up in Latin letters would be absurdly pretentious. The only reason I dare write to you in our language instead of French, as in all my other correspondence, is that I know you will judge me with leniency and kindness. One must dress appropriately: jargon must remain garbed in rabbinical characters, and must not dress up like a crow in peacock plumes. The writing system cannot be changed until the Spanish spoken and written here is the same as or similar to that of Spain. We should not try to hide that this would be a major reform.

If it is not inconvenient, could you please send me the issues of La Ilustración Española containing your articles? Many of my friends have heard me read them your letter to the youth of Vienna, and they were all filled with admiration and enthusiasm on hearing such noble words. In your letter to those young people, when you speak of the beauty of the Spanish language, you match form to content: I consider your letter a page of literature. Mr. Dalmedigo is taking the initiative to disseminate your articles here.

Warm regards. Your servant,

M. Fresco.

———•———

(Copy of Mr. Fresco's letter to Mr. Assens of Madrid:)

This language, which found favor in your eyes, is one that we consider a poor relative of the noble, rich lady that is your Spanish language: a poor relative in mended rags of different and varied cloths, unfit to be seen in good society.

[...]

I have no literary pretentions. I have had few occasions to write in Spanish, and if I decided to jot some lines to Mr. Pulido, it was because I could not resist: his kind words deserved some thanks, at the very least.

We were not taught Spanish at school, nor do we teach it to our children with books or courses, but it is passed down orally from parents to children.

Getting back to your articles, I should much appreciate if you could send me all of your published articles on this topic that so interests us. And if you wish to publish an article in Spanish newspapers here, that can be arranged. However, to make it legible to the general readership, it will be printed in the Hebrew alphabet. The papers here are "El Tiempo" and "El Telegrafo"; in Salonika, "La Epoca"; in Smyrna, "La Buena Esperanza" and others; in Bulgaria there are also three or four newspapers in our language, all in Hebrew letters. The readers of these newspapers do not know any European languages: those who know French or German read papers from France, Austria or Germany. This is why the Spanish newspapers must be written in Hebrew letters, as the readers do not know the Latin alphabet.

———•———

Constantinople, March 3, 1904.

Mr. Pulido:

Regarding your suggestion of printing our newspapers in the Latin alphabet, there is also the matter of spelling. Spanish spelling may be very simple, but getting it right still requires at least a little study or having read things in Spanish. Very few of our newspapermen have ever read a book from Spain, or have ever seen Spanish printed in Latin characters. And if they wished to write their articles in that alphabet, they would make horrible errors. What would you say if you saw the following Spanish words written this way: "Espagna, Tourquia, la enstrouction, el progresso"? Most of the journalists would write Spanish using French phonetics. Would it not give Spaniards more sorrow than pleasure to see your beautiful language disguised in that undignified, ridiculous way?

Therefore, I do not think the reform should begin with newspapers.

Fresco.

MOISES DAL MEDICO[1]

Colonel and chief interpreter, Ministry of the
Ottoman Imperial Fleet, Constantinople

Constantinople, February 27, 1904.

Dear esteemed sir:

I hasten to thank you sincerely for your kindness in
sending me the Spanish Senate transcript containing the
discussion of the Eastern Jews' Spanish. It was a true pleas-

---

[1] Moïse dal Medico (ca. 1848–1937): linguist, civil servant and journalist in Turkey, and longtime board member of the Jewish Community
Council of Constantinople. At the time of this book, he was the chief interpreter of the Ottoman Navy. Known mainly as a journalist, he also
wrote books for teachers of Turkish and French.

From the 1880s to 1930s, he often collaborated with the newspaper
editor David Fresco, with whom he translated a compendium of Ottoman laws and published Ladino-language periodicals, including the
newspaper *El Nacional* and the magazine *El Amigo de la Familia* (an illustrated weekly about history, geography and literature). Jointly, he and
David Fresco were the final editors of the respected Constantinople Jewish newspaper *El Tiempo* (published from 1871 to 1930). Dal Medico was
still working at the age of eighty-eight, as editor-in-chief of *La Boz de
Oriente*.

He was married to author Rosa de Yejeskel Gabay, best known for her
1871 etiquette book *La kortesiya o reglas del buen komportamyento*, which
advocated modern education for Jewish women while remaining rooted
in traditional gender roles and religion.

Some sources give Dal Medico's first name as Moís or Mose. His last
name is sometimes spelled Dalmedigo.

ure to read your statement and proposals, and those of the Count of San Bernardo.

This intriguing discussion convinced me that people in Spain are starting to notice the existence of a large number of her descendants whose ancestors lived the same life as their fellow Spaniards, shared their woes and joys, contributed to the glory of their shared country, and participated in the regeneration of the Spanish language.

Jews are not, as their enemies claim, pariahs, people without a country; on the contrary, they idolize the country that grants them hospitality, tolerance and equal treatment. They do not hesitate to assimilate into the population and contribute to their respective countries' welfare. In most European nations, Jewishness is merely a matter of religion: they are Englishmen in England, Frenchmen in France and Ottomans in Turkey. This sentiment, which you noted among the Jews in Vienna and elsewhere in Europe, tends only to improve the precarious situation of their brothers who still suffer for their religion in some regions.

In the East, where governments did not pressure populations to adopt the national language, people have preserved their respective tongues: the Jews use Spanish, the Greeks modern Greek, the Armenians modern Armenian.

It is natural that each of these peoples should feel a special love for the language they speak.

Personally, besides my love for Turkish, which I have learned well, and for literature, to which I contributed by publishing several works, I have had a lifelong predilection for Spanish. In fact, at age fifteen, I translated Genoveva from Greek into Spanish, and later a large number of novels from French. For several years, I edited a periodical called "El Amigo de la Familia" and the political newspaper "El Telegrafo." I have always enjoyed reading Spanish books more than French or other works.

I hope you will be pleased with the following information about the matter that so concerns and honors you:

1) Current state of the Spanish language in the East.

Very few Eastern Jews study Spanish. They absorb it through everyday use: *only a small number* try to speak and write it more or less correctly, thanks to the Spanish publications they read and the use of a dictionary and, only rarely, consultation of a grammar book.

There are, then, two categories of Spanish-speaking Jews: the ignorant and the educated. The former speak and write a Spanish dating from the century of Ferdinand and Isabella, corrupted and mixed with numerous words from Hebrew, Turkish and (in Servia and Bulgaria) Slavic.

The language also varies by country and province. In Salonika, for instance, they still use "facer" (to do) and "fijo" (son or child), while in other places they use "hacer" and "hijo"; in Salonika they say "ciuda" (city) and "bondad" (goodness), and in other places "civdad" and "buendad." Moreover, they use certain words whose etymology would be hard to trace. Examples include "meldad" (to read), "jara" (forest), "reda" (handkerchief), "aviamela" (female cousin), "pendola" (pen), etc., etc.

The educated—meaning those who know European languages, and particularly the editors of Judeo-Spanish newspapers and translators of novels and other books–avoid foreign words and seek to use only purely Spanish terms. However, they unwittingly make two major errors: they apply French pronunciation to Spanish words and they use a structure and style that, far from being Spanish, is more French or Italian.

I do not doubt that I, too, fall into this category.

2) The number of Jews who speak Spanish.

Spanish is spoken by all the Jews of European Turkey (besides the Vilayet of Janina, where they talk Greek), all the Jews of Asia Minor, Bulgaria and Servia, and by the Spanish Jews of Bucharest and Vienna.

The main Spanish-speaking population is as follows:

European Turkey		130,000
Asian Turkey		120,000
Bulgaria		30,000
Servia		5,000
Bucharest		2,000
	TOTAL	287,000

3) Prospect of Spanish disappearing from the East.

From my perspective, here is all that can be said about this prospect: Countries' efforts to promote their own language will not be enough to eradicate Spanish from the

East. If it happens, it will be because the Jews—practical people who give great importance to educating their young—wish to ensure their children's future. Studying French used to be enough to guarantee this, and therefore the Alliance Israélite founded numerous schools that taught entirely in French. However, amid extraordinary growth in trade relations between Germany and the East, Jewish children are flocking to German schools. In Pera, where I live, out of a Jewish school-aged population of one thousand, more than 400 children attend German schools.

Today's educated young people, ignorant of pure Spanish, use French in their literary, political and scientific discussions. Business correspondence occurs exclusively in German or French. Educated mothers do not want their children to speak Spanish but French or German.

Nonetheless, the prospect of Spanish vanishing is a matter of *longue haleine*, as the French say. It cannot disappear completely as long as families have even one member who does not know French.

We must also acknowledge that even families that know French still use Spanish in their intimate interactions.

In conclusion, because enlightened families avoid Spanish only out of a desire not to speak a corrupted language, I can state with conviction that if this language were taught in schools, it would undoubtedly be used in preference to French and German.

Such education must be handled very skillfully. My numerous responsibilities prevent my pursuing this project, so I refer you to Mr. Moise Fresco, Headmaster of the Alliance school in Galata, with whom you are already in touch, as he knows the subject well. Please do not mistake him for Mr. David Fresco, editor of El Tiempo, a worthy man in his own right.

With the utmost respect and esteem,

Moise dal Medico.[2]

P.S.: When time allows, I shall find you a sample of the Spanish language as it was written 30 to 35 years ago. This will show you how much the Alliance schools have helped to improve, or rather how they were the only factor that indirectly improved, our language in the East.

---

[2] **DAL MEDICO'S NOTE:** Old spelling: "del Medigo."

PINHAS ASAYAG[1]

Distinguished Spanish Jew in Tangier; a highly
cultured spirit, a great and decorated promoter of
Spanish interests, a journalist who writes in
proper, elegant Spanish. Correspondent for
the Madrid newspaper *El Liberal*.

Tangier, February 23, 1904.

DR. ANGEL PULIDO—MADRID.

Most respected and distinguished sir:
It was with indescribable delight that I received your
kind, much-appreciated letter of the 20th. Even before you

---

[1] Pinhas Asayag (fl. 1880s–1910s): acclaimed journalist in Tangier who
wrote for numerous Spanish periodicals, often under the pen name Veritas. He also wrote for some Sephardic papers in North Africa.

In 1889, Spain honored Asayag's work as a political correspondent by
making him a Knight of the Order of Isabella the Catholic. Granting
knighthoods to Jews marked a radical change for Spain, where just twenty
years earlier it had been illegal to practice any religion but Catholicism.

He was one of the few Jews who wrote to Pulido in modern Spanish,
rather than Ladino or French. In *Españoles sin patria...*, Pulido calls him
"one of the most appealing personalities we have ever met face to face,
beloved by all who deal with him." Asayag joined the board of the Jewish
Community of Tangier in the late 1800s and was still its secretary in 1917.

Though resident in Morocco and a devotee of Spain, he was a naturalized French citizen. French sources often spell his last name Assayag.

PINHAS ASAYAG
DEFENDER OF SPANISH INTERESTS IN TANGIER,
DECORATED BY THE SPANISH GOVERNMENT,
AND CORRESPONDENT FOR SEVERAL SPANISH NEWSPAPERS,
INCLUDING "EL LIBERAL"

wrote to me, I had carefully relished your beautiful letter published in *El Liberal*, addressed to *La Esperanza*, the Jewish association in Vienna.

It would be presumptuous of me to try to praise that beautiful document as it deserves, enumerating its many merits and lauding it from a literary, historical and social standpoint. I am too small and lacking in faculties for such a large undertaking. Suffice it to say that it has touched my every feeling, and as a Jew, I find it deeply moving to think that in Spain there are still eminent men of your stature who will outstretch a shielding hand and look with love and fellowship on this defenseless, libeled, persecuted race. You express yourself with a lofty perspective that honors you, and the sincere affection and respect with which you speak of the Jews inspires feelings of gratitude I am pleased to express, along with my admiration. Please accept my most cordial congratulations, which— though insignificant, being mine—are sincere and enthusiastic.

Your noble attitude and steadfast efforts to help the Jews regain their ancestral tongue deserve plaudits for their patriotic and humanitarian nature. They prove that Spain does not forget her children and that, amid her offspring's misfortunes, she comes to offer generous protection to make up for past rejections. I am so glad your attitudes toward the Jews echo those of the great Castelar, that king of Spanish oratory and a glory to all mankind, whom we Jews adore and venerate. We can never forget his brilliant defense of our race at the Constitutional Convention of 1869, in response to Canon Manterola.[2] When Castelar visited us in Tangier not many years ago, he was touched and pleasantly surprised to see a framed copy of that grandiloquent, wonderful speech, with his portrait at the beginning of it, on the front of our Community Hall. He said our gratitude moved him deeply, and he praised the local Jews' use of proper Spanish, which is their preferred language for expressing themselves both in business and at home. It can be said it is our language, though most of us know two or three others. The Jews of Tangier, Tetuan, Asilah, Larache, Alcazar, Mazagan, etc., etc. talk a Spanish of varying correctness, but still unquestionably Spanish, and of course purer than that of their fellow Jews in Turkey. Even the old people who write their correspondence in Hebrew letters do so in Spanish. Everything about us here is Spanish: our tastes, interests, impressions, enthusiasms and feelings. We are Spanish in vocation, temperament and sympathies. Spanish blood courses through our veins: we think in Spanish, feel in Spanish, say some of our prayers in Spanish. Our weddings follow the ritual established when the Jews lived

---

[2] Canon Vicente Manterola (1833–91): a priest elected to Spain's Constitutional Convention of 1869. He represented the Catholic Unity ticket, which had vowed to prevent religious freedom and to oppose separation of church and state. At the convention, he railed against secularism and against Jews.

In response, delegate Emilio Castelar (1832–99) defended religious freedom and touted the Jews' many contributions to Spain and the world. When the convention voted to include religious freedom in the Constitution, Canon Manterola walked out and boycotted almost all the remaining sessions. Castelar went on to become minister of state and, later, prime minister of Spain.

in Spain, and during the ceremony we read the bride's and groom's family tree, which refers to our forebears who died in Spain, and we ask God to *dé descanso a sus almas.*[3]

The Jews of Morocco, especially in Tangier and Tetuan, feel a special connection to Spain. All things Spanish interest us directly: we grieve her losses and celebrate her triumphs. She is our motherland, the blessed soil where our ancestors' remains rest, and it is natural we should feel affection and veneration for her. One wretched decree, one error of fanaticism, made her cast out this fine progeny, who would have enriched the country and avoided innumerable persecutions and miseries; but that is the past and there is no need to recall it. Fortunately, the Jews are glad to forget it, for they know not to confuse Inquisition-era Spain with twentieth-century Spain.

The Spanish-American War, to name just one example, highlighted the Jews' love for Spain and their strong desire to see the Spanish side—the side of justice—prevail.

The Alliance Israélite Universelle has established schools in Tangier, Tetuan, Larache, Fez, Meknes, Casablanca, Mogador, Marrakesh, etc. All offer young people a solid education, and although the schools give preference to teaching French, all of the students do learn Spanish.

People here are avid readers, and young people of both sexes follow Spain's intellectual movement closely. The Spanish press is unusually popular among us, and no one here is unfamiliar with all the Spanish politicians and their

---

[3] Rest their souls.

leanings. Politics exists here to an extent, but there are no professional politicians. Orators are admired and politicians are judged. Writers and poets well known among the Jews include Cervantes, Espronceda, Zorrilla, Castelar, Campoamor and Núñez de Arce. Novelists such as Fernández y González and Escrich were once very popular, and now the favorite authors are Galdós, Pereda, Blasco Ibáñez, Valera, Palacio Valdés, Pardo Bazán, etc. Playwrights include Echegaray, Dicenta, Benavente and Quintero.

I shall be happy if this information, written with little thought, interests you. I send warmest regards, with friendship that, though unfruitful, is wholesome and true. Affectionately,

Pinhas Asayag.

———•———

Tangier, March 2, 1904.

Dr. Angel Pulido—Madrid.

Dear esteemed friend:

Thank you so much for the sympathetic reception you saw fit to give my letter, whose only merit, after all, is sincerity. It was written from the heart and reflects my purified love and fervid sympathies for the Spanish nation: for that noble, generous Spain that was the cradle of our ancestors and which still holds, as sacred relics, the ashes of wise, illustrious men whose names we inherited. Your letter moves me to the utmost, and Mr. Vicenti, a truly wonderful person whom I am honored to count as a friend, is extremely benevolent to me. I thank you both for your favor. Mr. Vicenti was in Tangier and saw for himself how prevalent the Spanish spirit is among us, how we use Spanish at home and how we are in every way Spanish, heart and soul.

I certainly never imagined my insubstantial, poorly drafted letter to you could ever deserve the honor of publication. But if a good man like you thinks it worthy, you not only may publish it but may do so in any way you think will best suit and serve your patriotic project.

It may interest you to know that many Jews in Morocco have Spanish names and wear them with a certain legitimate pride, saying they come from Spain and are thus Spanish. There are families called Toledano, Laredo, Pariente, Pimienta, Lalio, Medina, Moreno, Perez, de Avila, Aragon, de Loga (Loja), Corcía (Garcia), Farache (Aznalfareche), and others too numerous to list.

I once met a good, learned Spaniard—a great patriot very familiar with Moroccan affairs—who made a proposal to the Spanish government on how to treat the Moroccan Jews. He suggested that, given the sizable Jewish presence on this side of the Strait and given the Jews' industriousness and influence in Morocco, Spain should *protect them all* and consider them political emigrants. However, the then Minister of State thought the idea too audacious and was frightened to consider it. Though it pains me to say so, I must point out that Spanish officialdom has not always requited the Moroccan Jews' feelings: the harder they strove to prove their attachment to and affection for Spain, the more that country responded with rejection or aversion.[4] This was blatant both before and after the famous Madrid Diplomatic Convention of 1880.[5] Spain and England led those negotiations, acting on reports and pleas from the Spanish minister at Tangier. By restricting Europe's rights in Morocco, they obliquely dealt a deathblow to Moroccan Jews who, to survive, must seek the protection of foreign flags. The conference limited the protection available to resident aliens, and the Moroccans were satisfied with their victory, thanks to the zeal and intervention of Spain's and England's representatives in Tangier.

Spain missed her chance. When she had more influence and power in Morocco, she could have attracted at least a large portion of the Jewish population. However, given her over-scrupulous consideration for Morocco, she could not or would not do this. Other more visionary nations, however, realizing Jews might become important figures in the future, welcomed them more benevolently.

To rectify Spain's misguided, self-defeating policy, Spanish representatives such as Mr. Ojeda and, currently, Mr.

---

[4] **PULIDO'S NOTE:** To judge how ill-conceived this behavior is, we refer the reader to the article from *Le Monde Illustré* at the end of this book.

[5] The Madrid Diplomatic Convention was an 1880 agreement between Morocco, the United States and a dozen European countries. It dealt primarily with foreign countries' protection of expatriates living in Morocco.

Cólogan, both very honorable people, have taken a different approach that is yielding successful results. They wisely realized it serves Spain's interests to follow a policy of attraction, and that even without commitments or large unauthorized initiatives, there is no reason to spurn a portion of the population that deserves respect and which is also addicted to Spain and spreads her language throughout the empire. Both Mr. Ojeda and Mr. Cólogan have made themselves popular in Morocco and much beloved by the Jews: the former left behind fond memories and the latter is well regarded and is highly esteemed and extolled for the exquisite propriety of everything he does.

Mr. Canalejas was here, and enjoys great popularity among the Jews, who admire him so. He was pleasantly surprised to hear Jews talking Spanish and to realize they all were familiar with his politics, with his split from Mr. Sagasta, with his beautiful, fiery, eloquent speeches that captivated and stirred the masses, and with his brilliant campaigns for democratic ideals.

Likewise, brave General Segura expressed enthusiasm for the welcome he received from the Jews, who expressed praise and admiration for his brilliant comportment in the Cuban jungle and for his fearless valor throughout the Cuban War.

He said he believed in Spain and that he had a better time here than he had imagined possible.

That valiant seaman Mr. Diaz Moreu also had occasion to see how the Jews here knew of his achievements in Santiago, Cuba and his heroic actions aboard the Cristobal Colón.

The distinguished journalist Saint-Aubin also got to see how popular his newspaper writings are here and how everyone here talked to him about his faithful "Stork."[6]

Many Spanish orators inspire enthusiasm among the Jews, and all their speeches are read here with true interest. Maura is widely admired, as are Moret, Canalejas, Salmeron, Silvela, Melquiades Alvarez, Pidal, Montero Rios, etc., etc. Moya's speech in defense of the press, in response to Maura, is widely celebrated and is deemed a real triumph for the worthy, enlightened Editor of "El Liberal."

People here consider Romero Robledo to be Spain's leading parliamentarian and they much appreciate his jokes in Congress. They celebrate Montero Rios as the leading jurist and canon law expert; Vega de Armijo as the greatest, most impartial Speaker of the Senate, a great gentleman, consistently democratic, of noble heart and lineage; Villaverde as a great public finance expert; and Melquiades Alvarez as a revelation and as Castelar's successor as an orator. Salmeron is admired for his austerity, his Catonism and his devastating eloquence. They consider Azcarate divine, a man out of his time, a rare find among politicians. His incomparable austerity, his blind faith in his principles, and the consistency of all his actions attract true admiration.

It would be easy to keep going on about Spain and the Jews, but I see I am laboring the point and do not wish to become a bore.

---

[6] Alejandro Saint-Aubin (1857–1916): Spanish journalist, critic and painter. Asayag mentions a stork because Saint-Aubin sometimes claimed to be publishing information that a helpful stork gave him.

I offer you this information, uncertain whether it will interest you, with the single goal of showing that the Jews here keep current on all things related to Spain, its men and its issues, and take a special interest in all matters Spanish.

If you wish to use any of this in your forthcoming booklet (assuming anything I wrote is worth bothering with) you may do so without asking. My only hope is that when you publish it, you will please favor me with a copy, as a memento of you.

With fond regards, I remain your faithful and affectionate servant and friend.

Pinhas Asayag.

———•———

Tangier, March 22, 1904.

Dr. Angel Pulido—Madrid.

My distinguished friend:

Your two lovely letters reached me promptly. I am sorry to learn that, for now, your commitments preclude your planned visit to Tangier, though I do not give up hope of seeing you here eventually. If you do visit, you know I shall be entirely at your disposal, to the extent that a humble, insignificant person may assist you.

I sent our community's Chief Rabbi the issue of "El Liberal" containing your beautiful, gallant letter to the Viennese Jewish organization, La Esperanza, confident that reading it would interest him as much as it delighted me. I was right: those brilliant paragraphs, filled with warmth and sincerity, with their vivid, eloquent sense of noble tolerance combined with healthy patriotism, in the best sense of that word, greatly impressed our highest rabbinical authority. He applauds and wholly appreciates your commendable efforts to promote and develop the sweet language of Cervantes among the Jews of Spanish descent. The illustrious Most Reverend Mordojay Bengio,[7] who is flattered and excited by anything that tends to extol and favor the Israelite flock, was intensely pleased to learn that a distinguished Spanish Senator and noble essayist, a man of your preeminent gifts, has raised his official voice in favor of a community that, far from forgetting its Spanish origin, boasts of it. He was elated to know you have offered the Jews your spon-

---

[7] Rabbi Mordecai Bengio (1825–1917): chief rabbi of Tangier for more than sixty years, from 1853 until his death.

Widely respected among Morocco's three major faiths, he maintained correspondence with Jewish leaders in many countries. Rabbi Bengio served as president of the Moroccan branch of the Anglo-Jewish Association (a group devoted to improving conditions for Jews in developing countries) and organized relief projects for Jewish refugees of the Spanish-Moroccan War. He also supported the era's Jewish educational reforms, whereby students learned secular subjects and professions alongside traditional religious studies.

Sources transcribe his first name variously as Mordajay, Mordecai, Mordechai, Mordo Chee, Mordochee or Mordojay. The spelling varies even within Asayag's letter, as published in Pulido's book.

taneous affection and heartfelt sympathies, striving to spread a thesis of unity and fraternity among the Spanish Jews, who are true brothers of Spain.

Be assured, dear Doctor and friend—for you became our friend when you had the happy inspiration to pursue this gratifying campaign—that the echoes of your affection go straight to our hearts, which value and give thanks for such unequivocal proof of ardent kindness.

The Chief Rabbi, like most Jews in Morocco, is also of Spanish descent and speaks Spanish. It is the language of his most solemn sermons and speeches, which are naturally rich in quotations from and references to Mosaic dogma, a field in which he is deeply erudite. An eloquent speaker, he produces oratory with ease and abundance. He is known for his splendid perorations and his oratorical imagery, always opportune, precise and tailored carefully to the situation.

Rev. Mordajay Bengio, considered one of the most learned rabbis in the West, is an enlightened person, a great theologian and eminent Talmudist. Despite his priestly nature, he is very tolerant and can mold his outlook perfectly to the century in which we live. He is much loved and respected by his flock, and is appreciated and highly regarded by local and foreign authorities, with whom he maintains the necessary relations.

With the Spanish legation in particular, he generally lives in perfect harmony.

Some years ago, we were visited by Mr. Francisco María Tubino, now deceased, editor of "La Andalucia" in Seville, who was a member of the San Fernando Royal Academy of Fine Arts. Like you, he had a fondness for the Spanish Jews and anything to do with their lives and history. He expressed a vehement desire to meet the Chief Rabbi, and I was very glad to arrange that.

We had a long visit in his home and Mr. Tubino was enchanted with the Chief Rabbi and with their interesting conversation on a variety of topics, especially about the Spanish Jews.

As a token of this, and as a souvenir of his visit to that honorable authority, the wise Spanish scholar gave the Jewish leader a beautiful book in which he wrote an affectionate inscription about the Jews of Spanish origin.

The Chief Rabbi treasures it.

The roster of eminent men who—like Castelar, Carvajal, Tubino and many others—distinguished themselves through their sympathies for the Jewish race must now also bear the illustrious name of the wise, renowned Dr. Angel Pulido. Like those others, he occupies a special place in our hearts and an indelible, pleasing memory in our mind.

Take care of yourself, my dear friend. A warm, fond handshake.

Yours truly,

Pinhas Asayag.

[4]

Parliamentary document

THE SPANISH SENATE
SESSION OF NOVEMBER 13, 1903

Mr. SPEAKER: Mr. Pulido has the floor.

Mr. PULIDO: Gentlemen, I requested the floor to address the Minister of State with an exhortation (I dare not call it anything else), whose importance will be clear once you hear me explain the reasons for it.

If I were addressing a Minister who was less youthful, less cultured, less well versed in public wealth and the manifestations of modern life, a Minister who, unlike you, did not generally know of events in other countries, then I should have taken the floor with trepidation. I should have feared that the exhortation I was about to present would seem trivial and trifling, and even, to some people, contemptible. However, the attributes I recognize in you let me trust that you will grant it the importance that I believe it has, and that I believe it merits.

I refer to the following: This summer I traveled through several nations of Southern Europe, venturing as far as Constantinople. I journeyed through some twelve to fourteen countries, and in all of them I witnessed a manifest desire, with accompanying actions, to have their national language flourish in other lands. In other words, I saw—for instance, in France, Germany and even England and elsewhere—the teaching of foreign tongues: people studied languages there and then took their own children to the countries where those languages are spoken, already speaking them on arrival, having studied them in their own nation. Conversely, I saw these same countries work to have their own language known and studied in other lands whose tongues they had made their own children learn, as I already mentioned. This has resulted in enormously fruitful relations that we have absolutely disregarded.

More specifically, I shall say that in many Eastern countries, I found Spanish alive and well. In Bucharest, Belgrade, Constantinople and other cities where I expected to have trouble communicating, we imagined we would have to draw on our French or German. These languages, however, were largely unnecessary, as Spanish is tremendously abundant there. It is unclear how many people in those nations speak Spanish: I know of no statistics that could tell us how many Spanish Jews in all those Eastern countries use this language in their personal lives and even in business. Nonetheless, I can assure you that they correctly consider

Spanish their own language, their native language, and in some places there is enormous interest in preserving it.

In certain cities, there are schools devoted to this purpose. In Bucharest, for example, there is a Jewish school, built recently at a cost of about 30,000 duros, in which some classes are taught in Spanish, particularly religious classes. Well, on July 25, they held exams there in which some students had to express themselves in various languages, reciting poetic compositions and reading bits of text aloud. Where Spanish is concerned, I am told that one of them read an original poem by the school's headmaster (Mr. Enrique Bejarano, a learned polyglot who knows a great many languages and is much respected in the East). I shall take the liberty of reading that poem here, as it is short, expressive of the style used in Eastern Spanish, much like our Old Spanish, and noteworthy, as it reflects a great love for our country and our language, which I think we would do well to appreciate.

It reads as follows:

THE SPANISH LANGUAGE

> Thou, holy language,
> Thee I adore,
> More than all silver,
> More than all gold.
> Thou art the most beauteous
> Language;
> To thee all fields of knowledge
> Give every advantage.

Through thee we talk
To God above,
Lord of the Universe
And of Nature.

Although my holy people
Has been captive,
Through thee, my beloved,
It was consoled.

And I know that when this heartfelt composition was read there before the gathered crowd, evoking memories of the Mother Country, and, above all, exalting the Spanish language, people wept and were moved deeply, which proves their affection for this language of ours, which that race has preserved across the centuries.

In other words, Mr. Minister, I observed two important realities abroad: first, every cultured nation considers its own language a sort of testament to its sovereignty and an aspect of its public wealth. Therefore, Italy, Germany and England seek to propagate their language in other lands.

In Udine, I attended a conference whose primary aims included founding an Italian-language university in Trieste; I saw efforts to establish French-language schools and a French university in Greece and Beirut, and saw French publications and periodicals in Constantinople and Bucharest, the Roumanian capital, which attest to the sovereignty France still exerts there through its language, to the point where some courses are taught in French. And I have seen how those nations do everything possible not just to maintain their linguistic foothold in those capital cities, but to expand it. They understand, as I indicated, that this is not only a testament to a country's intellectual sovereignty, but a factor or sign of its public wealth, which can be—and is being—used to more positive ends, including, principally, commercial trade interests.

The second fact I observed is that we, because of extremely well-known events in our history, have more than half a million individuals scattered across every country of the East who use our language, about which they care deeply, but whom we regard with utter disdain. We neglect them so thoroughly that we are unaware of their Spanish publications and, as far as I know, not even the Academy of the Language has deigned to contact them to make one or more of them a corresponding member. As far as I can tell, in the countries of Southern and Eastern Europe that I am discussing, the Academy has only one corresponding member in Vienna and one in Budapest, who surely were named for reasons wholly unrelated to this type of knowledge. In short, we have averted our eyes so completely that we are not even curious about how they express themselves in Spanish, and they are likewise equally ignorant of us, as Spanish books do not circulate among them, and it is extremely rare to see a Spanish book in those places.

I wish to draw the Minister of State's attention to something I learned of in Turkey, thanks to a conversation with Dr. Elías Pasha, one of the Sultan's physicians, with whom I spoke in Spanish, for he is a Spanish Jew: the potential disappearance of his language. I asked this illustrious doctor if he had a family, and he said yes, that he had children he was sending to university. I also asked if his children spoke Spanish, and he answered, "No, my children no longer speak Spanish. They use English and French." So at least in that family, the Spanish language is being lost. These days there is a pitched competition among languages, to promote their study and use, and countries that protect their own interests pay attention to this important matter. They promote their language through schools (we have ample evidence in Madrid and throughout Spain) and through publications, seeking to have it prevail, spread and overtake other tongues, including, if possible, the national language. In this competition, given the natural consequences or logical outcomes of the battle, Spanish might gradually disappear from those parts of the world in favor of other languages deemed more useful and cultured. And in a way, we shall have contributed by completely ignoring this vital issue.

I do not know whether this brief outline gave you a sense of the matter's importance, but I believe it to have great relevance: as you well know, we wish to export our products to as many places as possible and enhance our relations with all other countries. Unquestionably, the surest, most positive, essential, necessary way to build such relations is through our language. If we have numerous Spanish speakers in those places, including cities like Salonika where Spanish is the dominant language, I now ask you what I previously asked myself: Is the Spanish government willing to view this with indifference and utter disdain, or is it willing to act? What could the Spanish government do? These are the questions that immediately occur to anyone. You might think of many points that do not occur to me, but in any case, I think that if I were in your position, I should do something. Different approaches might come to mind, but naturally I should consider it essential for the consuls to provide the Ministry of State with information about the Spanish Jews in all those countries of the East, to find out how large a population we are discussing; and to study their use of Spanish and the kind of publications they have, so that we could become familiar with the essentially Spanish organizations and printed matter that exist in those places. We should keep in mind that many of the organizations founded there (including one established recently in Vienna) are defined by their Spanishness. In other words, they take pains to make it a defining feature of the organization: they are Spanish in nature and aim to study the Spanish tongue and strengthen ties among people of Spanish origin, for they consider themselves Spaniards. That is the only term they use to describe themselves: Spaniards of the East.

So, then, gathering that information would be my first step. Second, I should ensure that our consuls in those places can speak Spanish. Not all of them do, and there have been cases where, for example, a town with a large number of Spanish speakers is served by a consul who does not initially know the language. And then I should do something else: gather all these documents and all the information about the forms of Spanish expression that exist among the peoples of the East, and I should send them to the Minister of Public Education so he could forward them to the Academy of the Language. I believe the Academy of the Language should take very great interest in this matter, should look upon it with some affection, and should first of all implement whatever suitable prizes and educational programs it deems appropriate, in an attempt to: 1) ensure the preservation of Spanish in those parts of the world, and 2) have it differ from our own language as little as possible. By this I mean having it sound as it would if not for the effects of time that separate these languages more each day, until they will become completely different tongues in a more or less remote future.

Establishing relations, nurturing them and, as much as possible, opening literary communication so they understand how warm it makes us feel to know they use our language: this strikes me as a project for the Academy of the Language. Such actions would warrant applause from every Spaniard, and would, in the short or long term, benefit Spain in ways more positive than mere cultural exchange. If language now seems just a literary concern, a moment's thought makes clear that it affects other, more important interests. We therefore must preserve, promote and spread the former so that it can serve as the channel through which to preserve, promote and spread the latter.

That is what I wished to tell you: as you can see, what I am presenting is not a plea but an exhortation, so that once you have heard it, you may assess it as you see fit.

THE COUNT OF CASA-VALENCIA: I request the floor.

Mr. SPEAKER: You have the floor.

THE COUNT OF CASA-VALENCIA: I requested it to correct some inadvertent errors that our honorable colleague, whom it was a pleasure to hear, made about the Spanish Academy. The Academy concerns itself constantly and intently with all aspects of preserving and spreading the Spanish language.

You said the Academy has hardly any corresponding members in other countries, and this error needs correcting. The Spanish Academy has important and numerous corresponding members in Paris, London, Berlin, Vienna, Rome, Dublin, Bucharest, Cologne, Warsaw, Washington, Strasbourg, Holland, Lisbon, Oporto, Louvain and other cities, and corresponding members in nearly all the Spanish American republics. The Academy maintains extremely close relations with them, to the point where those countries' Academies consult the Spanish one when they are asked questions about the language.

Spanish is widely spoken and disseminated. As you surely know, for some years now, Spanish has been a compulsory subject at the University of Bordeaux. There is a situation in London that benefits Spain: besides knowing international law, the history of treaties and other subjects, anyone taking the test to join the diplomatic corps there must speak French, German, and another language chosen by the candidate. Well, for some years now, nearly all candidates have chosen Spanish, for a very simple reason: since England has an embassy and legations in Spain and in the sixteen Spanish American republics, that language would let them serve in any of those legations, whereas learning Russian enables them to go only to St. Petersburg; Italian, to Italy; and Portuguese, to Rio de Janeiro or Lisbon.

You were perfectly right to say that in Constantinople's Jewish Quarter, only Spanish is spoken. I have conferred with someone who has been there for some time, who told me it is truly curious to hear them speak Spanish, as it is the Spanish of the late 1400s, when they were expelled from Spain; that they publish a newspaper written in Spanish, printed in the Hebrew alphabet, and I have in my possession a copy of the New Testament, paid for by those Jews, printed in Spanish and, again, in Hebrew letters.

Mr. PULIDO: I request the floor.

Mr. SPEAKER: You have the floor.

Mr. PULIDO: I wish to inform the Count of Casa-Valencia that he has not corrected anything I said. There was nothing to correct, as we are in agreement: when I complained that the Academy had no corresponding members, I was not referring to all foreign countries but only the nations of Eastern Europe.

I have studied the institution's list of corresponding members in every part of the world, name by name, to see which were in Eastern and Southern Europe. Surely you would agree that the Academy has no correspondents in

Bucharest or Salonika or Adrianople or Philippopolis or Constantinople or Belgrade or in many other places I need not list one after the other, which are precisely where we can find the largest concentration of these Spanish Jews, who use our language in their own fashion.

In this part of Eastern and Central Europe, the Academy has but two corresponding members, as I said: one in Vienna and one in Budapest. Vienna has few Spanish Jews. Budapest has more, but fewer than other cities. Where this community is thriving and developing is just beyond those locales, especially in places such as Salonika, where Spanish is the dominant language.

The Count of Casa-Valencia confirmed what I had already pointed out: in Bordeaux, in Germany and in England, they do teach Spanish, but only to advance their own interests. They do not reach out to serve our interests but so that we will serve theirs. In other words, they want to ensure that their native citizens who must emigrate to Spanish-speaking countries will know Spanish, just as they aim to have people in their own country know the local language: not Spanish in that case, but English in England, French in France and German in Germany, through initiatives that they hope will prove profitable. This is what I wish to call to the government's attention.

Therefore, to make the same point you just presented, absolutely the same point, with which I fully agree, for you did not in the least contradict anything that I had the honor to tell this body, I shall address the Minister of State. Now that my comments are corroborated by no less an authority than the Count of Casa-Valencia, please understand that this is quite an important matter, and it would be worth half an hour of your time on one of the days when you are at the Ministry. It deserves handling with the energy that characterizes your approach to international affairs. For the reasons that I pointed out and for others that I omitted in order to keep this exhortation within regulatory length, please believe that this matter of the Spanish language deserves and should receive attention from our consuls, the Ministry of State and, by referral, the Academy of the Language, as I already indicated.

THE COUNT OF CASA-VALENCIA: I request the floor.

Mr. SPEAKER: You have the floor.

THE COUNT OF CASA-VALENCIA: I requested the floor earlier because I thought I heard you say the Spanish Academy had hardly any corresponding members in European countries. That is why I said it has correspondents in almost every European capital. As for the countries you mentioned, I shall say that our consistent custom is not to appoint people: to avoid snubs, we name only people who have requested membership, and then, with the greatest pleasure, we grant the title of corresponding member.

THE MINISTER OF STATE (Count of San Bernardo): I request the floor.

Mr. SPEAKER: You have the floor.

THE MINISTER OF STATE (Count of San Bernardo): It has been a true pleasure to hear the words of my dear personal friend, Mr. Pulido, and, except for the first part, which was motivated purely by his kindness to me, I agree completely and absolutely with his assessment of these matters.

You mentioned one idea that is already under consideration. You rightly said it is best not to have consuls abroad who do not know Spanish. I feel so strongly about this that I just had the honor to read a bill in Congress to reorganize the consular service, establishing two requirements: 1) to know proper Spanish, and 2) to speak the language of the country in which he resides.

As you see, the current Minister of State is already moving things in that direction.

Regarding the effects of language knowledge on every facet of life, especially our trade relations: Why should I bother the Senate with lengthy disquisitions? The statistics you were good enough to suggest compiling sound useful. I shall personally do what I can to find out who the people are who for centuries have spoken the beautiful language of Cervantes in the Eastern countries, and also (within the usual paltry budget of a Minister of State) see if, in places with a large concentration of Spanish speakers, even if they are Jewish, we can manage to have a school established to keep alive the core of the beautiful Spanish language. I yield the floor.

Mr. PULIDO: I request the floor.

Mr. SPEAKER: You have the floor.

Mr. PULIDO: I thank the Minister of State for the response he was good enough to give me.

I expected no less. Because you are a cultivated person, I knew you would immediately grasp this topic that we tend to look at askance, though it makes such a strong impression on Spaniards who travel abroad.

I can assure you of one thing: people in those parts of the world will appreciate anything our government may do. Whether this means taking time to send them books or showing interest in their Spanish-language publications, it will inspire infinite gratitude and deep emotions. You see, I cannot forget that while traveling on the Danube on two separate occasions—once twenty years ago and once this summer—I heard various people from Sofia, Adrianople and Philippopolis, and others from Bucharest and Belgrade, as I was saying, I heard them speak of Spain with such intense emotion and a shudder of pleasure and adoration, with tears in their eyes, recalling times past, and I heard them speak to other Spaniards in their language.

Therefore, since in some places Spanish Jews have indicated a desire to regenerate their speech and since, as I told you, in Vienna they recently tried to form a Society of Spanish Jews to promote such work and such studies, I am sure that if the Academy of the Language takes the initiative to name some corresponding members, and if the Minister of State sends some of our books to Spanish-Jewish schools— books of any genre—the Jews would lovingly study our Spain, our riches and our interests, and you can be certain that this would yield very fruitful results. It would not only build ties, which is always useful, but our commercial agents and proxies would also find opportunities that might not exist at present, given certain rifts or a lack of relations. Once communications are established, I believe that everyone will benefit.

Therefore, I conclude by thanking you again, Mr. Minister, for the way you have responded to the exhortation that I had the honor to present.

[5]

Diplomatic precedents

Note on the repatriation of Spanish Jews in 1881[1]

In response to Russia's expulsion[2] of the Jews, decreed in 1881, many Hebrews petitioned the Spanish Ministers in

---

[1] **PULIDO'S NOTE:** By courtesy of the Marquis of Vega de Armijo and the relevant department of the Ministry of State.

[2] What happened to the Jews of the Russian Empire starting in the early 1880s (and continuing well into the twentieth century) is best described as persecution rather than outright expulsion. An expansion of brutal anti-Jewish laws coincided with outbreaks of mob violence against Jews (from 1881 to 1884 alone there were hundreds of pogroms). Restrictions on where Jews could live, what they could own, what professions they could practice, and their access to education and to elected office grew ever more stringent. By 1891 and 1892, when Russia expelled twenty thousand Jews from Moscow and banned most Jews from that city, a large percentage of the empire's Jewish population had fled or was fleeing to other parts of the world. A great many, however, stayed there, either by choice or because they lacked the resources to leave.

St. Petersburg and Constantinople for aid in coming to Spain. The Ministers referred those requests to the then Minister of State, the Marquis of Vega de Armijo, who replied with the following Royal Order, sent by telegraph on June 15 of that year:

> His Majesty has charged me to tell Your Excellencies that both His Majesty and the Government will welcome the Hebrews from Russia, opening to them the doors of their former homeland.

This consent, published not only in the newspapers of Constantinople and St. Petersburg but also in those of Servia and Bulgaria, produced excellent effects, according to those Ministers.

The Minister at Constantinople, the Count of Rascón, also said that the Spanish government's noble consent could greatly benefit our country's trade. He reasoned that if the expelled Jews settled along Spain's Mediterranean coast, they would establish communication with the more than three hundred thousand Jews of Spanish origin who speak our language perfectly and who earn a living in commerce or trade, who could consume our agricultural products previously shipped to them under a foreign flag. He proposed establishing a regular steamship line from Seville to Odessa and founding a Spanish secondary school in Constantinople, similar to Germany's Royal Schools, and another in Salonika.

On June 25, this same Minister—after acknowledging and describing the educational level of Jews in Turkey, and after citing publications such as the Spanish-Jewish newspaper *El Telégrafo* and a monthly magazine recently begun by an organization called La Esperanza—asked to have some collections of books sent to them. This was done, the request having been forwarded to the Ministry of Public Works and Education on July 4 of that year.

When the Balkan States refused to admit Jews and when the German Empire took steps to deprive them of citizenship rights, the Spanish government reiterated its offer on June 17 of that year.

The government could not defray the costs of repatriating Spanish Jews, but it negotiated free transportation for fifty-one people and a considerable discount on the transportation of many more, who, assisted in Marseilles by the Spanish Consul (the Marquis of González), arrived in Barcelona in September of that year.

Later, in 1891, Jews in Odessa again requested repatriation to Spain. The Spanish Minister in Russia conveyed this request, dated December 31. The Spanish government responded with the Royal Order of January 27, 1892, which cited the measures and offers proffered ten years earlier, and again indicated that they could come to Spain, whose laws ensured freedom of worship.

The Royal Order
MENTIONED ABOVE

To the Minister Plenipotentiary of Spain at St. Petersburg.
Madrid, January 27, 1892

Your Excellency:

Apprised of Your Excellency's dispatch in which, at the request of some Jews living in Odessa, you asked if His Majesty's Government would let them settle somewhere within the Monarchy, the Minister of State asked us to inform Your Excellency, so you may notify the interested parties, as was done in 1881 through the Spanish legation at Constantinople, that the Nation's laws in no way bar foreigners from settling on the Peninsula if they so desire, as and when they wish, with the knowledge that these same laws guarantee them complete and absolute freedom of conscience, as they do for anyone not professing the Catholic faith, and therefore they need no special authorization to come to the Kingdom, which they are free to enter without obstruction; but that what cannot be done is to provide aid to transport them here, as our Budgets do not allow this. — From the Royal Order conveyed by the Minister of State, which I am quoting for Your Excellency's information.

*Message from the Count of Rascón dated June 16, 1881, acknowl-
edging receipt of the Minister of State's telegram informing the
Count of the resolution made by His Majesty the King (may
God protect Him) about Jews fleeing from the Russian Empire:*

"I shall convey its content to the Jewish Committee that
has come to this city," says the Spanish Minister, "and shall
try to provide the means for them to take advantage of the
offer made by His Majesty's Government, this most noble,
generous offer that can benefit the Spanish Nation im-
mensely."

[6]

The French language among the Jews of the East

THE ARTICLES IN THIS BOOK had been written and almost all had appeared in *La Ilustración Española* when we received issue 2,402 of the Parisian weekly magazine *Le Monde Illustré* (April 11, 1903). Mr. Rousso of Constantinople, whom we thank for his assistance in our work, sent the magazine and other interesting information. We opened this elegant, renowned publication and, under the headline LA LANGUE FRANÇAISE EN ORIENT: ŒUVRE SCOLAIRE DE L'ALLIANCE ISRAÉLITE, we found a long article illustrated with twelve photogravures and two maps. We had scarcely begun reading it when we felt deep stirrings that grew as we progressed through the text. It was a fascinating account of what France is doing to win over the race of Jews spread across the East, mostly of Spanish origin, and to sway them to devotion and service to France's intellectual and material interests. We originally planned to excerpt the article. However, all of it seemed so important and instructive that—for fear of distorting it and losing much of its value, and since we considered it a serious alarm bell that maps out a line of political action for our country—it seemed our great patriotic duty to reprint it intact and bring it to the attention of Spanish statesmen, consuls, academy members and writers. I urge you all to read it and notice how other countries are reaping the strength and richness that we, in typical Spanish fashion, abandoned. We have italicized the most revealing passages.

THE FRENCH LANGUAGE IN THE EAST
The Educational Work of the Alliance Israélite[1]

It looks best from a distance, in the great silence and vast peace of the desert: the silky Sea of Gennesaret, nestled mysteriously in a hollow among the iridescent mountains, dominated by the snowy cap of Mt. Hermon. The still surface of the water is an intense azure that holds your eye, and the pale-blue sky itself looks so deep that it could be another lake, stretched miraculously between the peaks.

Far below, the white, ramshackle buildings and the low domes and scraggy palm trees of Tiberias are a blurred speck on the tide-foamed coast. On bare rocks that bulge along the shores, the light casts indescribably magical decorations, unexpected chromatic contrasts, harsh notes, jarring tones that delight and disconcert.

But as we descend the steepening slopes towards the shabby town that hides behind crumbling towers and black basalt walls, not even the persistent magical light can help: neither the lake's allure nor the sky's radiant splendor can overcome the immense dreariness of the dilapidation and the ruins. Customs, traditions, beliefs: everything here is

---

[1] Translated into English from the original French. Pulido's book omits a few sentences, which appear as notes in this edition.

Quercus, the French journalist who wrote this article, suffused his writings with scorn for Orthodox Jews and for traditionalist Muslims. A staunch colonialist, he disparaged non-European cultures while touting the superiority of all things French. Nonetheless, amid his editorializing here, he presents a rare, vivid portrait of Jewish educational projects in the Middle East, circa 1900.

old, amid the unspeakable ancientness of all things Eastern. Like Jerusalem, like nearby Safed, Tiberias is a holy city in which the old persists and where Jewish particularism finds one of its last refuges. Aiming to be less vulnerable than in the Zion of the prophets, Jewish immigration brings ever-larger numbers back to this place. Even if nothing remains of the ancient Herodian city, the contours are there, perpetuated twenty centuries later by a race that lived its bravest hour here, a race that could easily have been crushed forever beneath the "harsh flatting-mill of the Roman world."

Those who come to die in this necropolis tend to be stubborn obscurantists. Like their ancestors who rejected Greco-Latin thought, they resist our western culture by erecting a barrier of furious fanaticism and staunch distrust. The willful ignorance in which they bask is truly frightful. They are prisoners of the past, pinned down by the weight of tradition. They close ranks, cutting themselves off from the world, walled in by ritual, observance and the ghetto. Behold it in all its horror: the intolerant Judea of ages past!

Nonetheless, in this anti-secular milieu, in this far-off Tiberias, isolated between two deserts and seemingly buried in the deep Jordan River basin, travelers *now have the surprise of hearing our clear French syllables ring from the lips of children.* In mazes of alleys where little white, cube-shaped Oriental homes squeeze irregularly into alveoli, and in covered bazaars where the acrid scent of spices mingles with the stench of the street, urchins swarm around, chirping our language as easily as they speak their own. This is because a few years ago, the Alliance Israélite Universelle founded a boys' school and a girls' school here, amid a mummified community. The Alliance modeled the schools on its other institutions in the East, and now we see the result of these first efforts. The boys' school opened in 1897 and the girls' in October 1900. Before that, Tiberias, like most communities in Palestine and Syria, had known nothing but Talmud-Torahs run by grimy rabbis, in which boys squatting on mats struggled to learn to decipher the Hebrew alphabet. Levantine towns are crawling with Talmud-Torahs, alongside countless prayer halls frequented devoutly by zealots of the Law. It is, in a way, the counterpart of the Arab madrasa, where poor youngsters, under a long stick held by a sheik, exhaust themselves by endlessly reciting suras from the Koran.

Creating schools in these environments, which meant colliding head-first with entrenched religious prejudices, seemed the most chimerical of enterprises twenty years ago. Nearly everywhere, the rabbi excommunicated the educator, the *apikoros*, and his impure knowledge. The fight went on, but the breach had been made and school triumphed decisively over synagogue. We can assess the resulting intellectual improvement, for which our French language was the effective tool, simply by walking through any Alliance school and then, as a point of contrast, visiting the best-run Talmud-Torah. Readers who compare the two photographs printed here—the old-fashioned school and the modern one—will see the unmistakable difference.

TALMUD-TORAH
OLD-STYLE JEWISH PRIMARY SCHOOL

FACING PAGE:

MODERN SCHOOL
ONE OF THE ALLIANCE ISRAÉLITE SCHOOLS

Sometimes, teachers have had to work absolute wonders to do their job. In Tiberias, for instance, the headmaster, Mr. Hochberg, found the whole population roused against him by the rabbis, and had to promise the families not to teach anything but Hebrew.[2] The school did, in fact, teach Hebrew, but it served as a vehicle for other subjects in the curriculum. This experienced, admirably patient educator *strove to awaken the children's minds gradually, to instill the desire to learn.* The Hebrew lesson became a science course, a history course, a moral philosophy course. And *then one day, while discussing history, he spoke to them about France, of her* deeds in the world, of her language, which is that of Europe's cultured elite, *the true language of civilization.* A useful language in Syria, where it is spoken in all the large coastal cities. And *he announced that if any student wanted French lessons, he would give them for free in the evenings, after class, on his own time. At first, just one student ventured to attend, then two, then three, then a proper small class who were soon envied as a privileged group. And finally, even the parents, who were Sephardim (Spanish Jews), came to ask the teacher to give their children French lessons. Thus Talmudic rigidity began to bend. The school introduced a regular course in its first division and, little by little, over several months, French became the language of instruction in all subjects except, of course, religious studies, entrusted to a rabbi. That is the system used in all Alliance schools. They won the battle so thoroughly that when the girls' school opened three years later,*

---

[2] Omitted sentence: "He made a kind of truce with the least inflexible locals, and a nucleus of students developed."

the families put up no resistance: from the first day, the headmistress and teachers used only French.

I asked questions while visiting this little world. Not only did the children understand all my queries, but the accuracy and confidence of their answers were striking. *How proud they all were to show a Frenchman the progress they had made!* They vied to see who would raise a hand to go to the blackboard, the terrible blackboard that our Western pupils too often consider an instrument of torture.

The classroom facilities are well designed: well-ventilated rooms whose walls bear maps, natural-history pictures and *all manner of special illustrations that, like the books placed in the children's hands, come from our best-known Parisian publishing houses.* Of the 120 boys who attend this school, 70 eat lunch there. To give them a taste for working the land, the headmaster teaches a basic gardening course, complemented by practical sessions on a plot of ground rented for this purpose. The best students go on to the vocational school in Jerusalem or to the Mikveh Agricultural School. Others are apprenticed to artisans: coppersmiths, blacksmiths, saddlers, wheelwrights, carpenters, etc., etc., whom the Alliance pays a small sum to train them. And so the effort continues: *French thus moves from classroom to workshop,* and this manual labor is meant to round out the intellectual and moral education begun at the school.

Though newer, the girls' school already has 200 students. Combined with the enrollment of the boys' school, that makes 320 pupils out of Tiberias' 4,000 Jewish residents, a very large percentage.

The girls' school is in a separate, very well laid out building. All classrooms open into an interior covered gallery in the Moorish style, and the windows face the lake. The most pleasant, sunny room is reserved for the littlest girls, out of health concerns for which the young, intelligent headmistress cannot be praised enough. About eighty little girls, the poorest, use the canteen, where they receive a hot meal at midday. The curriculum is the same as at the boys' school. Their manual apprenticeship is in sewing. All the little girls are extremely diligent: the worst punishment that can be imposed on those who neglect the rules of cleanliness is to send them home for a day. You should see how immaculate they are and what a contrast they are from the other children of Tiberias, whose eyes and noses are too often nests for flies.[3] Curiously, it seems these little curly heads contain more independence than is seen in the boys. The girls whom I asked about arithmetic, for instance, did not hesitate to draw the + sign, a cross, while at the boys' school they replace it with an inverted T: ⊥. I do think a thin voice whispered, "It's a sin." But so timidly!

These childish reactions show how petty and low the primitive fanaticism of these lands can be. In this regard, I should note that *of the two elements that make up the Jewish populace—the Ashkenazim, of German, Polish or Russian descent, and the Sephardim, who came to the East after their expulsion*

---

[3] Omitted sentence: "They already reflect the happy influence of their education."

PATIO OF THE JEWISH GIRLS' SCHOOL
DAMASCUS, SYRIA

from Spain—it is the latter who, practically all by themselves, make up the Alliance's entire school population in Palestine and Syria.

I cite the schools of Tiberias as an example because they are the newest and were set up in an environment unhospitable to our language and to the educational successes that flow in every way from our French methods. In towns less isolated and less closed to outside influence, the results are marvelous. I visited the schools in Jerusalem, Jaffa, Haifa, Beirut, Damascus, etc., etc., and can state that everywhere, the work of the Alliance Israélite remains unrivaled in its structure, the quality of its staff, and the education it provides. This sentiment is shared by all impartial travelers who are directly or indirectly concerned with the question.

The Alliance schools in Jerusalem have the largest enrollment in that city. They have huge new buildings with space for up to five hundred students, and a vocational school that I shall discuss shortly, the only institution of its kind in Palestine. Here as elsewhere, what is remarkable is how fluently the children speak our language. *In their mouths, French ceases to be a foreign tongue: they have assimilated it completely and talk it with stunning ease of diction. They use it constantly, not only in class and at recess but on the streets. They read books only in French, and one can say they have a French mentality. They love France wholeheartedly, know her history, especially her modern history, whose milestones include the emancipation of their race. I have seen fifteen-year-olds become choked up, their eyes wet with tears, at the mention of our country's glorious battles against old Europe for the triumph of justice, toleration and liberty.* This is precious because it indicates plainly the spirit of the education they receive, their intellectual training, thanks to distinguished educators such as Mr. Calmy, whom I must commend for his skill, enlightened dedication and impeccably sound methods.

Regrettably, there is no longer a Jewish French school for girls in Jerusalem. *Many girls have left the English school, as they only want to learn French, and they search in vain for teachers.* One hopes this gap will be filled and that there will be absolute equality of the two sexes.

Such equality does exist in the other cities in Palestine and Syria. In Haifa, for instance, the girls' school is on the same premises as the boys' school, and by the upper years these girls have acquired a purity of pronunciation that completely astonished me. This establishment, serving a hundred students, is overseen by Miss Delfour,[4] a refined, distinguished young Parisian Jewess, from whom *the children acquire diction that successfully sets aside the French patois* that too often grates on the ears in this country. I had them read difficult passages of prose or verse from an anthology, and they got through it wonderfully. It should be noted, though, that the girls everywhere have clearer, purer pronunciation than the boys. Of the latter, 191 attend the school in Haifa directed by Mr. Benchimol, whose lapels blossom with medals from the French government for his service to education.

---

[4] Historical staff records on the website of the AIU's archives give her name as Alice Dufour, not Delfour. See Bibliography for more information on the Alliance personnel records.

Along this Asian coastline, from the Sea of Marmora to the outermost bounds of Palestine, the Alliance Israélite has twenty-eight clusters of schools that teach some six thousand children in total. If we include comparable establishments in Morocco, Algeria, Tunisia, Tripolitania, Egypt, European Turkey, Bulgaria and Persia, the elementary schools alone number 112, educating more than thirty thousand students at an annual expense of almost 1.2 million francs, paid entirely by the Alliance. *This vast educational enterprise, from which France's cultural influence profits considerably,* does not, in fact, cost a single centime from our national budget.[5]

Although these schools were founded specifically for the Jewish communities, their doors are fully open to children of other faiths. Seated side by side with Jewish classmates, one finds Moslem, Greek Orthodox and sometimes Druse children, as in Haifa, where no fewer than thirty-five non-Jews attend the boys' school. It is to the teachers' credit that no proselytizing occurs inside or outside the classroom. This is an absolutely exceptional, very happy example in a country where racial antagonisms and religious hatreds are, as a tactical matter, expertly maintained and developed.

After graduation, the alumni have a role to play through private initiatives. Alliance alumni associations are proliferating and some are very prosperous. The association in Smyrna, for instance, can already donate three hundred francs to fund the popular evening courses in that city.

---

[5] Omitted sentence: "That detail is worth emphasizing."

These organizations generally have a library and reading room that, *besides the Alliance's regular publications, receive several Paris newspapers and some French magazines. There are periodic lectures and also theatrical performances* that invariably draw on our classical or modern repertoire.

———•———

The Alliance recruits its teachers from these same Eastern schools. Each year, the best students compete to go to the Jewish Teachers' College in Paris. Young women earn their certificate at three private boarding schools, where, like the young men at the Oriental Teachers' College, they receive instruction from French university faculty. In both cases, the curriculum is meant to prepare them for the advanced professional diploma, which most Alliance teachers now hold.

This ensures an absolutely consistent faculty. Uniform teacher training; uniform curricula, methods and spirit; in short, a unity of management from a central administration in Paris. It is the source of the unimpeachable superiority of the Alliance Israélite schools over all similar establishments.

I have kept the foregoing summary brief, since an exhaustive treatment would require a detailed, overly long monograph. It remains for me to say a word, now, about the two prototypes that are the Alliance's crowning achievements: its Vocational School in Jerusalem and the Mikveh Agricultural School near Jaffa.

The Jerusalem Vocational School is thriving today under the technical direction of a graduate from our Châlons School of Applied Arts and Crafts. Here the young are passionate about manual labor and understand its grandeur and beauty. Behold the man of the new generation, the Jewish laborer at last, clad in a leather apron, face blackened, chest exposed, sleeves rolled up over well-muscled arms. Such a fine replacement for the pitiful figures of the ghetto, the Biblical curled sidelocks, the hideous fur caps and the antediluvian long coats! The busiest workshops are the blacksmith shops: they employ thirty-seven apprentices supervised by a French foreman. The carpentry shop has twenty-six apprentices, the coppersmith shop twenty-one, the sculpture and woodcarving shop thirteen. Those are followed by stonecutters, woodturners, cabinetmakers, cartwrights, saddlers, etc., and finally the weaving workshops, where mostly Yemenites work. The sculpture and carving section is of particular interest. It is entrusted to Mr. Ben-Sion, an artist of merit who studied at our Paris School of Fine Arts.

Of the 115 students, 68 live on the premises. After their apprenticeship, they return to their country of origin or move to one of the big cities along the coast, where their specialty can guarantee them work. Teachers from the elementary school tutor the student apprentices each evening. This remarkable institution's general operating costs total 125,000 francs per year, minus about 48,000 francs in revenue from the workshops' products. The Alliance makes up the deficit of 77,000 francs.

PREVIOUS PAGE:
JERUSALEM VOCATIONAL SCHOOL
THE FORGE

FACING PAGE:
MIKVEH AGRICULTURAL SCHOOL
THRESHING MACHINE

The Mikveh Agricultural School was founded in 1870, patterned after France's *écoles pratiques*.[6] Its goal is not to produce specialists but colonists. Given the subjects it teaches and the nature of the courses, it can be considered an institution of higher learning. The program lasts five years, of which the first three are devoted mainly to theoretical instruction. In the final two years, students primarily do practical work, with lectures in the evening. No fewer than two hundred students live at the school. Like the director, Mr. Niégo, who is an excellent administrator, all the faculty he has brought together are graduates of our agricultural colleges: Montpellier, Versailles or Grignon. *It is such a center of French influence that our language is even beginning to spread among the Arabs in the vicinity.*

In 1870, this entire Plain of Sharon was nothing but sandy desert, but now it is a magnificent oasis, visited regularly by travelers passing through Jaffa. It is practical proof of the country's latent natural riches, which can be developed everywhere through European scientific techniques.

Intellectually and physically, everything here bears the mark of France. The books and tools come from France. The most advanced farm equipment systems—plows, mechanical mowers and reapers, reaper-binders, motorized threshers, etc. —are all made in our country. The French brand is also on the hand implements, supplies, hides, cloth, etc. Laboratory

---

[6] At the time, France's agricultural Practical Schools taught basic and intermediate farming skills, mixing classroom instruction with hands-on experience.

chemicals, groceries, fabric for students' clothing, hosiery, etc., are dispatched by French firms.

Like all Alliance establishments, it has a library consisting almost entirely of French works. Here is a random sampling of the authors whose works I found in students' hands during my visit to Mikveh: Corneille, Racine, Lamartine, Balzac, Flaubert, Sully-Prudhomme, Daudet, Loti, Bourget, Zola. Among the young people whom I questioned about their reading, I found a very well-developed literary judgment.

Upon graduation, the students are placed in Jewish colonies in Palestine or Syria as head gardeners, administrators or senior husbandrymen. Others are sent to colonies in Cyprus or Smyrna, or to farming settlements in Judea, Samaria or the Galilee. Those with the best grades go to the National Agricultural Institute in Paris, where they sit in on classes. During their stay, they reside at the Jewish Teachers' College in Auteuil.

Mikveh therefore grows and nurtures an elite youth with strong intellectual ties to France. While working towards its defined goal, the institution also happens to help maintain our cultural supremacy over the peoples of the Orient. Moreover, our consular agents in Palestine, who are no fools, have never shown the slightest sign of practical appreciation towards the School's staff or the School itself.[7]

One more important detail: to date, the Mikveh School has cost fully a million francs, which includes, it is true, the

---

[7] **PULIDO'S NOTE:** A reliable source assures us that in many places, our consuls still view Spanish Jews with marked disdain. If this is true, we must fight it energetically and indignantly.

price of the land, buildings, equipment, etc. The annual expenses total 163,000 francs, and working the land produces revenue of about 65,000 francs. That leaves a deficit of 98,000, covered by the Alliance.

In short, then, Jewish educational work in Palestine, Syria and Asia Minor has three facets: 1) primary schools and apprenticeships; 2) a vocational school of arts and crafts; 3) an agricultural college. *There is a whole series of coordinated efforts*, and it would be impolitic and unfair to ignore them. In a recent article in the *Revue des Deux-Mondes* (the first issue for March), Mr. Anatole Leroy-Beaulieu, while calling the Jewish schools "one of the sturdy boughs from which the teaching of French branches across the East," frames his homage in these terms: *"In Eastern Europe, Asia, Africa and throughout the Mediterranean, the Alliance Israélite Universelle performs services to the French language that our patriotism should be able to appreciate, but which sectarian minds cannot recognize."*[8]

---

[8] The quotations are from Anatole Leroy-Beaulieu, "Les congrégations religieuses: le protectorat catholique et l'influence française au dehors," *Revue des Deux Mondes*, March 1, 1903, 70–113.

The full quotations read:

"To close the schools in France where the Alliance Israélite trains its teachers—where young men and women train for their mission, gathered from all the countries of the East to learn our language and our methods—would mean cutting from our hands one of the sturdy boughs from which the teaching of French branches across the East."

"In Eastern Europe, Asia, Africa and especially throughout the Mediterranean, the Alliance Israélite Universelle in particular performs services to the French language that our patriotism should be

The Alliance's educational work is not, however, the only thing the Jewish world has done in the Levant. There has also been a strong economic impetus for several reasons, especially since the influx of Russian Jews into Palestine. I wish to speak of these ongoing colonization endeavors that, thanks to massive French capital, have spread some twenty farming communities from the plains of Ashkelon to the mountainous regions of central Syria. This return to the land for the physical and intellectual uplift of the race has left a forceful imprint on the progress of Jewish thought over the last twenty-five years. The three groups of colonies—Palestine, Samaria and Galilee—have settled a population of five thousand souls on this soil. Other settlements are forming in the Trans-Jordan region, near the Haouran, where vast swaths of land have recently been acquired. We find these efforts all the more interesting as *they are the only attempts thus far to counter the German colonization efforts.* I visited the largest agricultural colonies and was astounded at the determination, labor and courage it took all these pioneers to realize their dream. In the scorching sand and on once-bare rocks, there now grow vines and trees. Fields of grain wave as far as the eye can see in a place where before, even thickets would not creep. Marshes were drained

---

able to appreciate, but which sectarian minds are unable to recognize."

Anatole Leroy-Beaulieu, who wrote extensively about international affairs in the late 1800s and early 1900s, was also the author of the 1905 booklet *Les immigrants juifs et le judaïsme aux États-Unis,* which the Between Wanderings collection has published in English as a photo book called *Jewish Immigrants in Early 1900s America: A Visitor's Account.*

to stem the fevers that had carried off whole families. They have dug wells, built canals and erected villages that, amid the arid surroundings, are true havens of greenery. Schools, libraries, lecture halls, elected municipal governments: it is European life flowering in the middle of the desert.

The Jewish colonists have succeeded mainly as wine-growers. With the aid of plans from Bordeaux, they have set up magnificent vineyards that yield a superior wine.

The layout of their cellar at Rishon-le-Zion was more or less copied from the Girondin system. A grave crisis, over-production and sales at a loss, led to a necessary response: the colonists are now expanding their efforts into large-scale farming and into raising livestock.

Whatever happens, they are a force to reckon with from now on. In their transformation, the Jews are casting off their shackles, taking on a modern appearance and mentality, and, more and better than some others, they can serve as a link between Europe and the East. They have already introduced a new type of agriculture here, and they are likely to bring industry to the region as well. *Our rivals understand this, no doubt, as this clientele, which is very much ours, is being fought over bitterly.*

All of England's propaganda or would-be propaganda is directed at the Jewish element, but with an eye to religious proselytizing that, very fortunately, limits its effects.[9]

---

[9] Quercus was writing at a time when European colonial powers were competing for cultural and commercial dominance over the Middle East. In the previous paragraph, he says that France is winning the fight (Middle Eastern people are "this clientele, which is very much ours"). He

Germany, despite the anti-Semitism it exhibits at home, delights in the promises its emperor made to the Zionist delegation during his journey to the Holy Land. Could there have been more than promises, since, at the Zionist Congresses in Basel, there was majority support for motions recognizing the German sovereign?[10]

Lastly, Russia, which decreed stern measures against its subjects of the Mosaic faith and corralled them into Bessarabia and along Russia's western border, has now ordered its consuls general to extend its protection to all Russian Jews in Palestine and Syria— protection most of them would gladly do without.

Let us not forget, though, that these Russian Jews make up most of the population of the agricultural colonies, founded with French capital and run by a French administration.

That suffices to show us what policies to pursue and what role to play.[11]

QUERCUS

---

knows that Britain, too, is courting the Jews of Palestine, but he thinks the British will undermine their own efforts by trying to convert people to Christianity, thus alienating the Jews.

[10] Omitted sentence: "On this topic, let us say that the Zionists are the Alliance's adversaries for reasons that cannot concern us, as they relate to the inner aspects of Jewish life."

[11] **PULIDO'S NOTE:** And in light of these very eloquent French, German and Russian pleas and arrangements designed to win over these Jews, mostly of Spanish origin, we ask the reader: What is Spain doing? What are her consuls offering? Disdain, if not contempt. O sad country! O miserable class of ambassadors, ministers and consuls, who have not yet been able to leave behind ancient, clichéd prejudices and enmities!

[7]

1902 Budget of the Alliance Israélite

We reproduce the following from the *Bulletin de l'Alliance*, as we consider it interesting.[1]

---

[1] Numeric typographical errors in the Spanish book have been corrected to match the budget as published in the 1902 edition of the *Bulletin de l'Alliance Israélite Universelle*.

RECEIPTS	Francs
Membership dues	160,989.36
Donations to general operating fund	5,159.80
Miscellaneous income	830,522.57
Income to the Reserve Fund	13,796.18
Miscellaneous grants for the schools	52,506.25
" from Jewish Colonization Assoc.	267,000.00
" from Tunisian government	10,000.00
Lifetime membership dues	22,968.50
	1,362,942.66

EXPENDITURES	Francs
Girls' preparatory school	54,674.20
Boys' and girls' primary schools	551,959.38
Food and clothing	80,996.53
Secondary schools and higher-education institutions	14,199.70
Boys' apprenticeships in the East	75,568.30
Girls' apprenticeships in the East	21,226.15
Vocational school in Jerusalem	65,178.43
Agricultural school in Jaffa	90,392.05
Farm-school in Djedeida	92,395.50
Miscellaneous allocations and grants	5,190.80
Library	3,480.40

Printing	14,765.15
Postage	5,288.85
Rent	7,483.20
Miscellaneous expenses	61,907.99
School real estate	204,203.85
Payment into reserve fund	13,796.18
Lifetime membership dues paid into capital	22,968.50

	1,385,675.16

Expenditures	**1,385,675.16**
Receipts	**1,362,942.66**
Deficit *paid from capital*	**22,732.50**

[8]

Mr. Zayas' report

ON PAGE 23, WE MENTIONED a report written by Mr. Antonio de Zayas in Constantinople about the current social, political and mercantile status of Jews residing in the Ottoman Empire, the Kingdom of Roumania and the Principality of Bulgaria. We were able to obtain a copy of this interesting but short document (twenty-two pages of tight lettering). Aside from its poor coverage of the Spanish Jews' social status, the rest is valuable. The summary table at the back of the report is important, and we transcribe it below:

CITIES	Jewish pop.	Spanish-Jewish pop.	Under Spain's protection	COMMERCE
Constantinople	60,000	52,000	200	Imports from Austria, England, France, Germany and Persia. Export of tapestries and embroidery.
Salonika	50,000	50,000	320	Imports and exports are in Jewish hands.
Smyrna	25,000	22,000	30	Export of fruit. Import of tapestries from Persia, which they then export abroad.
Adrianople	15,000	14,500	138	Export of grains.
Dardanelles	3,500	3,500	25	Export of grains.
Gallipoli	1,600	1,600	22	Import of manufactured goods.
Rodosto	1,500	1,500	2	Export of grains.
Kavala	700	700	3	Export of grains.

WORSHIP	EDUCATION	PRESS
32 synagogues.	13 Alliance Israélite schools and 38 community schools.	*El Telégrafo*, daily, and *El Tiempo*, weekly.
36 synagogues.	1 Alliance school, 4 community schools and 4 private schools.	*La Época*, weekly.
9 synagogues.	2 Alliance schools, 2 community schools and 4 private schools.	*La Buena Esperanza*, *El Novelista* and *El Melleret*, all weekly.
5 synagogues.	2 Alliance schools, 1 community school, 1 private school and a rabbinical seminary.	None.
3 synagogues.	2 Alliance schools.	None.
2 synagogues.	1 community school.	None.
2 synagogues.	1 community school.	None.
2 synagogues.	1 community school.	None.

[9]

Addendum: Letter from La Esperanza

THE REST OF THIS volume was already in print when we received this very interesting letter, in which the young intellectual segment of the Spanish-Jewish people, gathered at universities in Vienna, answers our letter published in *El Liberal*, which we also reprinted in this book. The document's importance led us to include it here as an addendum.

MORITZ LEVY
PHILOSOPHY STUDENT, SECRETARY OF THE
SPANISH-JEWISH SOCIETY *LA ESPERANZA*, VIENNA

"ESPERANZA."
Academic Society of Spanish Jews in Vienna
IX-Türkenstrasse-8.

Vienna, April 5, 1904.

Health and peace to the revered senator representing the University of Salamanca, Mr. Angel Pulido in Madrid.

Dear sir:

Your loving, ardent letter to us in the Feb. 17, 1904 issue of "El Liberal" impressed and excited the hearts of La Esperanza's young members more than our words can express.

These feelings survive in our hearts like embers of a great fire in a hearth, now covered in ash but revived in our memory by the spirit of your warm, thrilling words. To describe these feelings and give your friendly greeting the response it warrants, we would need your eloquence and deep knowledge of Spanish, rather than our jargon, which barely gives us the expressions needed for everyday mundane conversations.

Your esteemed son, who read your article to us one night on your behalf, saw the great enthusiasm that your friendly, noble letter produced in us. He witnessed the emphatic cheering and loud, spontaneous applause when he finished reading it.

Honored sir: Ever since our ancestors were banished from Spain, it has been very rare for a Spanish-Jewish group, or even a Spanish-Jewish individual, to have the chance to come into contact with a Spaniard and address the serious issue of the Spanish Jews' position in the East with regard to Spain.

The Esperanza academic society feels cherished and lucky to have attracted the attention of an illustrious gentleman such as you. It therefore seems right to share our feelings with you frankly.

In your journey through the cities of the East, you must have had many occasions to discuss this with Spanish Jews of greater age and authority, but we entreat you to hear the opinion of our youth as well.

Different Spanish Jews have different feelings toward Spain: the feelings of liberal men who know of their ancestors' brilliant past in Spain, and the feelings of our less educated people.

The former admire the high culture and progress of their forebears in Spain, and avidly study that period of Spanish history in which their ancestors played such a role in literature and knowledge, especially in Spanish-Jewish knowledge and poetry, from the Moorish occupation until 1492, the year of the expulsion. There is ample proof that they hold no grudge against Spain, and that their hearts swell with sadness at the memory of those long-ago times. Please forgive our brief historical digression.

The Jews whom Spain banished were forced to appeal like mendicants to the hearts of the era's generous sovereigns, begging for asylum where their families might rest after the terrible expulsion. They were thus scattered across various countries in Europe, Asia and Africa. The proclamation by King Ferdinand of Aragon and Queen Isabella ordering the Jews to leave their country was a deathblow to the sciences and literature they had been cultivating there. In Spain these Jews had been centralized in one country and could work together with their compatriots for cultural and scientific advancement. In exile, dispersed to the four corners of the world, with a few of them here and a few there, that body's arteries of life and knowledge and culture were severed, the body torn to pieces and each piece left on its own.

These poor, destiny-tossed expatriates found refuge in countries bereft of education, in cities in North Africa, Turkey, Asia Minor and elsewhere, which were thus several centuries behind in culture, science and literature, which the Jews brought with them from their country.

Even Jews who took shelter in the European provinces of the Turkish kingdom, despite some toleration, had to suffer under the terrible blow of exile. These poor people were forced to battle for their painful existence, leaving no surplus time for learning. Persecuted so cruelly by fate, the Spanish Jews of Turkey nonetheless made superhuman efforts to maintain the high culture of their ancestors in Spain, but for natural reasons, they did not succeed. The dispersion into small groups in different provinces of the Turkish kingdom, the primitive nature of the nations in which they settled, the need to learn a new language and the ways and customs of a new country into which they needed to assimilate to some extent—all these formed a major obstacle to sustaining what they had brought from Spain. Thus only in the first decades of the 1500s were the Spanish Jews of Turkey able to maintain their high level of culture. What followed was the Spanish Jews' darkest period. A harsh slumber and a long, four-century lethargy fell over their intellectual capacities! Only in the second half of the 19th century did the Spanish Jews in Turkey, Roumania, Bulgaria and Servia, and in Asia Minor, Egypt and Algeria, begin some trial projects focused on science and the fine arts, thanks to various sources of help and influence (the Alliance Israélite Universelle).

Thinking of those four sterile centuries, those hundreds of years lacking in any intellectual production, the heart of any enlightened Spanish Jew would swell with sadness, mourning for his past. Yes, this was the most terrible blow of the miserable exile under which some groups of Spanish Jews still suffer in the East.

Their heart does feel sadness, but no antipathy or revolt against modern Spain. Just the opposite. They even consider themselves fortunate if happenstance brings them into contact with a Spaniard, whom they treat as an old acquaintance, earnestly asking after the current state of things in Spain and listening admiringly to the sweetest, most beautiful, most harmonious language on Earth. The names of Seville, Granada and others that they hear—intelligible words first heard in childhood in sweet ballads and old songs in the pure Spanish language, with whose tender melodies their grandmothers sang them to sleep in their arms—bring sweet recollections of those times.

These ballads and songs are our only mementos of Spain and of pure Spanish, and even they are unfortunately disappearing.

Oh, how much displeasure an enlightened man feels and how it hurts his literary and intellectual development to be unable to explain his sweet childhood memories, to not be in a position to put his fantasy into words and speak in his own mother tongue!... Through no fault of our own, our mother tongue was reduced to a completely unpoetic jargon, and we think its regeneration is almost impossible for natural reasons: lack of contact with its original wellspring.

Your letter to our Society salutes and praises our efforts and our attempts to regenerate our ancestral language. Actually, on several occasions, guided by sacred feelings for our beautiful language, La Esperanza did use circulars and pamphlets to agitate publicly, with all our might, for the regeneration of our language. Sadly, we must report that our efforts did not succeed. The obstacles are too great for our limited strength to combat.

Educating a people as large as ours requires well-organized schools, requires literature and requires lively contact with the source from which that language flows. But for reasons both political and practical, the Spanish Jews of the East must fight for their existence with the same weapons as their neighbors, which means learning the national language in earliest childhood. And so our mother tongue is abandoned. La Esperanza therefore is compelled to focus its preliminary activities on its own members.

As for our people in general, curiously they see their jargon as belonging exclusively to their nation, so if you ask them what language they speak, they will say "Judío" ("Jewish"). Besides using words and expressions that modern Spanish considers archaic or dated, their language is rife with terms and expressions borrowed from the foreign languages of the countries where Spanish Jews reside. In your journey through the East, for example, you must have heard this for yourself straight from the people's mouths.

Today, the only things the Spanish Jews of the East retain from their old Spanish homeland are the name "Spanish Jews" and their error-laden language.

Let us summarize. We counted ourselves lucky that our ancestors, as peaceful inhabitants, were once allowed to work with their fellow Spaniards to advance culture and knowledge, and that we can follow their glorious example by making a point to preserve our Jewish nature. However, though they were innocents cruelly wounded by fate, it is our lot to toil energetically, wherever we may live, for the progress and rights of our Jewish nation and for its revitalization. The board of our organization urges each member of La Esperanza to work toward that goal once they return to their country after graduation and enter into contact with their people.

Before we close this reply, please accept our profound thanks for your warm, caring, friendly message to our society. It will always stay fresh in our memories. Our organization is pleased and grateful for your benevolent offer of modern Spanish books. Please accept our best regards to you and to your son, who is our good friend. With all our heart, we wish our old homeland prosperity, progress and glory!

We hope you will see fit to continue your warm feelings toward our society.

With respect and affection,

ON BEHALF OF THE BOARD

	For the president
THE SECRETARY	THE VICE PRESIDENT
MORIS LEVY	B. ALCALAY
Philosophy Student.	Medical Student.[1]

---

[1] Moritz Levy (1879–1942) would become the Sephardic chief rabbi of Bosnia in 1917 and would later direct a rabbinical seminary in his native Sarajevo.

Orphaned at birth, he showed academic promise as a boy. This led a local Sephardic charity to pay for his university education in Vienna, where he earned a doctorate in Semitic philology in 1906 and where he was ordained as a rabbi the next year. His dissertation formed the basis for his 1911 book, *Die Sephardim in Bosnien* (The Sephardim in Bosnia).

Levy's election as Sephardic chief rabbi filled a post that had been vacant for over a decade. According to Rabbi Solomon Gaon, who studied under him, Levy was "the first university-trained rabbi in Sarajevo." Levy remained a community leader and Jewish educator until May 1941, shortly after the Nazis occupied the city. He died in the Holocaust. Historical sources give his first name variously as Moric, Moris, Moritz, Maurice, Moise, Moshe or Mose, and some give his last name as Levi.

"B. Alcalay" was the future Rabbi Isaac Alcalay (1882–1978), according to a 2013 history of La Esperanza written by Ayala and von Schmädel, and according to Freidenreich's 1979 book *The Jews of Yugoslavia*. Alcalay and Levy attended the Vienna Rabbinical Seminary at the same time and,

P.S.: We trust you will excuse the long, unpleasant delay in answering your much-appreciated letter to us. It took so long because of issues that arose in our organization after our costume ball last month.

---

over the next few decades, would work together on several Jewish projects. Rabbi Alcalay later served as the chief rabbi of Serbia, as a Serbian government envoy to the United States, as the chief rabbi of Yugoslavia, and as a member of the Yugoslav parliament. From 1943 to 1968, he was the chief rabbi of the Central Sephardic Jewish Community of America.

Bibliography

The following were useful in preparing the translation and notes.

1. LANGUAGE REFERENCE

(Besides Spanish-English dictionaries from the era)

Gil, Rodolfo. *Romancero judeo-español*. Madrid: Imprenta Alemana, 1911. A collection of old Judeo-Spanish ballads. Throughout the book, Gil annotates and glosses obscure Ladino terms. The book also includes a Ladino-to-Spanish glossary.

Jerusalmi, Isaac. "Ladino-English Glossary of Select Lexical Terms," an appendix to *The Song of Songs in the Targumic Tradition: Vocalized Aramaic Text with Facing English Translation and Ladino Versions*, 309–44. Cincinnati: Ladino Books, 1993.

———. "Ladino/Hebrew/Turkish-English Glossary," an appendix to *A Jewish Voice from Ottoman Salonica: the Ladino Memoir of Sa'adi Besalel a-Levi* by Sa'adi Besalel a-Levi, 299–355. Stanford: Stanford, 2012.

Kohen, Elli and Dahlia Kohen-Gordon, *Ladino-English English-Ladino Concise Encyclopedic Dictionary (Judeo-Spanish)*. New York: Hippocrene Brooke, 2000.

Orgun, Güler, Ricardo Portal, Antonio Ruiz Tinoco, et al. "Diksionario de Ladinokomunita: Djudeo-Espanyol <> Castellano <> English <> Türkçe." Accessed May 20, 2016.

http://ladinokomunita.tallerdetinoco.org/. A terminology database.

Pascual Recuero, Pascual. *Diccionario básico ladino-español*. Barcelona: Riopiedras, 1977. A small Ladino-Spanish dictionary.

Schmidt, Darrell Peter. "A Descriptive Comparison of Sephardic Spanish with Modern Spanish." MA thesis, Kansas State University, 1967. The back of the thesis includes a long list of Ladino terms paired with their Spanish equivalents.

2. HISTORICAL REFERENCE

(A partial list of sources consulted)

"Academia Española." *El Liberal*, June 11, 1904, 3. Coverage of Rabbi Bejarano's appointment as a corresponding member of the Spanish Royal Academy.

Álvarez-Sierra, J. "En el centenario del doctor Pulido." *ABC*, June 26, 1952, 9. A look back at Dr. Pulido's life, on the centennial of his birth.

Archives of the Alliance Israélite Universelle, online catalog. Accessed June 16, 2015. http://archives-aiu.org/aiu/index.htm. Includes historical personnel records of the AIU schools, useful in reconstructing the careers of the numerous educators profiled in this book.

Ayala, Amor, and Stephanie von Schmädel. "Viena y sus estudiantes sefardíes: la Sociedad Académica 'Esperanza' (siglos XIX y XX)." *Ladinar* VII–VIII (2013): 21–36. A well-documented history of the Sephardic student organization La Esperanza from 1896 to 1924.

Borovaya, Olga. *Modern Ladino Culture: Press, Belles Lettres, and Theater in the Late Ottoman Empire*. Bloomington: Indiana University Press, 2012. Provides detailed information about Ladino newspapers in the Ottoman Empire.

Bunis, David. "Modernization and the Language Question among Judezmo-Speaking Sephardim of the Ottoman Empire." In *Sephardi and Middle Eastern Jewries: History and Culture in the Modern Era*, edited by Harvey E. Goldberg, 226–39. Bloomington: Indiana University Press, 1996. Explores the changing status of Ladino in Sephardic communities of the late nineteenth and early twentieth century, and the pressures to replace it with other languages.

———. "Linguistic Conservatism: Judezmo Speakers on 'Old' and 'New' Language." In *Around the Point: Studies in Jewish Literature and Culture in Multiple Languages*, edited by Hillel Weiss, Roman Katsman and Ber Kotlerman, 135–81. Newcastle upon Tyne: Cambridge Scholars Publishing, 2014. A fascinating look at linguistic conservatism versus language change in Ladino. Includes a quotation from Rabbi Eliahu Crispin (page 162), explaining why his newspaper *El Luzero de la Pasensia* used the Latin alphabet.

Centre de la Culture Judéo-Marocaine. Website of a research and cultural center in Brussels, whose online holdings include scans of letters from the 1910s addressed to Pinhas Asayag as secretary of the Jewish Community of Tangier. Accessed July 3, 2015. Home page: http://www.judaisme-marocain.org.

Cohen, Julia Phillips, and Sarah Abrevaya Stein. "Sephardic Scholarly Worlds: Toward a Novel Geography of Modern Jewish History." *Jewish Quarterly Review* 100, no. 3 (2010) 349–84. Includes brief background information on Rabbi Moritz Levy.

Conder, C.R., H. H. Kitchener, et al. *Samaria*, vol. 2 of *The Survey of Western Palestine: Memoirs of the Topography, Orography, Hydrography and Archaeology.* London: Palestine Exploration Fund, 1882. See especially page 256 for information on the Mikveh Israel agricultural school, including where the land came from, the financial arrangements with the Ottoman government, and conflicts with existing Muslim and Jewish inhabitants of the region.

Danon, Abraham. *Recueil des romances judeo-espagnoles chantées en Turquie.* Serialized in *Revue des études juives*, 32 (1896): 102–23, 263–75 and 33 (1896): 122–39, 255–68. Rabbi Danon's anthology of old ballads sung by Sephardim in Turkey.

"Foreign News." *Reform Advocate*, August 24, 1912, 54. News item about Rabbi Bejarano's receipt of the Order of the Medjidieh medal.

Franco, M. [Moïse]. *Essai sur l'histoire des israélites de l'Empire Ottoman depuis les origines jusqu'a nos jours.* Paris: Librairie

Durlacher, 1897. Pulido draws heavily on Rabbi Franco's history of the Jews in the Ottoman Empire.

Freidenreich, Harriet Pass. *The Jews of Yugoslavia*. Philadelphia: Jewish Publication Society, 1979. Includes background on Rabbi Isaac Alcalay and Rabbi Moric (Moritz) Levy and their involvement in La Esperanza.

Gaon, Solomon. "Sarajevo as I Knew It." *Tradition* 30, no. 1 (1995) 30–37. Includes extensive background on Rabbi Maurice (Moritz) Levy, who had been Rabbi Gaon's teacher at the seminary in Sarajevo. Originally presented as a lecture at Congregation Shearith Israel in 1984.

Ginio, Alisa Meyuhas. "El encuentro del senador español Dr. Ángel Pulido Fernández con los judíos del Norte de Marruecos." *El Presente: Estudios Sobre la Cultura Sefardí* 2 (2008) 111–25. An article about Pulido's interaction with Northern Moroccan Jews.

Gourdji, S. Letter to the editor. *Archives israélites*, February 7, 1901, 44. Mentions the reelection of both Isaac Pasha and Moïse dal Medico to the board of the Jewish Community Council of Constantinople.

Hemeroteca Digital, Biblioteca Nacional de España. Accessed June 16, 2015. http://hemerotecadigital.bne.es/index.vm. Full-text digital archive of Spanish periodicals from 1683 to the present, including, among other relevant sources, the Madrid newspaper *El Liberal* (which printed numerous articles by Pulido or about him or his family, and letters from some of his Jewish correspondents) and *La Ilustración Española y Americana* (in which the first half of this book originated as a series of articles).

Historical Jewish Press, National Library of Israel. Accessed June 16, 2015. http://web.nli.org.il/sites/JPress/English/Pages/AllJPressPage.aspx. Full-text database of historical Jewish newspapers from more than a dozen countries. Invaluable in reconstructing biographical details of people in the book.

"Institutions charitables à l'étranger." *Archives israélites*, April 24, 1879, 138. Summarizes the 1877–78 financial report of the Bucharest Sephardic Primary Schools Society, with a list of its board members (including the Ascher brothers) and information on the schools' funding.

Israel Garzón, Jacobo. "El doctor Pulido y los sefardíes," introduction to *Los israelitas españoles y el idioma castellano* by Ángel Pulido Fernández, ix-xxv. Barcelona: Riopiedras Ediciones, 1992. An overview of Pulido's pro-Sephardic campaign, in a 1992 edition of this book.

The Jewish Chronicle online archive. Accessed June 16, 2015. http://website.thejc.com/archlnk.aspx. Full-text archive of this British Jewish newspaper from 1841 to the present. A useful source of information about people, organizations and institutions mentioned in this book.

Jewish Telegraphic Agency online archive. Accessed June 16, 2015. http://www.jta.org. Searchable articles from the JTA, a news service that has covered Jewish news since 1917.

Kayserling, M. *Biblioteca española-portugueza-judaica*. Strasbourg: Charles J. Turner, 1890. In *Sephardic Jews and the*

Spanish Language, Pulido cites and quotes this extensive biographical dictionary of Sephardic authors. It spans many centuries and concludes with a collection of old proverbs.

Laredo, Isaac. *Memorias de un viejo tangerino.* Madrid: C. Bermejo, Impresor. 1935. Photo-illustrated memoir of a longtime journalist in Morocco who served on the board of the Tangier Jewish Community alongside fellow reporter Pinhas Asayag. Several sections of the book deal with prominent members of that city's Jewish community, including Asayag.

"Nouvelles diverses." *L'univers israélite,* August 22, 1905, 760–61. Obituary of Moscu Ascher, describing his many educational and philanthropic activities. Translated into French from an obituary in the Romanian periodical *Egalitatea.*

Papo, Joseph M. *Sephardim in Twentieth Century America.* San Jose: Pelé Yoetz Books, 1987. Information about Rabbi Isaac Alcalay can be found throughout the book. See in particular the biographical sketch of him on pages 330–33, which includes information about his education in Vienna.

Popvici, Ileana, ed. *Evreii din România în secolul XX: 1900–1920: fast şi nefast într-un răstimp istoric: documente şi mărturii.* 2 vols. Bucharest: Editura Hasefer. 2003. A 1,100-page compilation of primary-source documents from Romania's Jewish communities, covering the years 1900–20. It includes considerable documentation of the Bucharest Sephardic community.

Pulido Fernández, Ángel. *Españoles sin patria y la raza sefardí.* Madrid: Establecimiento Tipográfico de E. Teodoro, 1905. Pulido's follow-up book includes further correspondence and more biographical details about people who appear in *Sephardic Jews and the Spanish Language,* and material from many other correspondents.

Rousso, Daoud. "Discours de Me Daoud Rousso." *Bulletin de "L'amicale" Association des anciens élèves de l'Alliance Israélite Universelle,* September 1910, 59–65. Rousso's speech in praise of the AIU schools, given at a 1910 alumni event. This AIU alumni magazine published the speech in the original Ottoman Turkish, followed by a French translation.

Simon Schama. *The Story of the Jews: Finding the Words, 1000 BC–1492 AD.* New York: Ecco, 2013. Includes information about the Jews in Spain before the expulsion.

Sigaléa, Robert. *De Bucarest à Sieugues: ou le chemin des écoliers et les sentiers de la peur.* Félines: Editions du Fayet, 2003. A memoir by one of Rabbi Bejarano's grandsons. It provides details about the rabbi's life not found elsewhere, and information about the 1880s–90s renovation of the Great Spanish Temple in Bucharest.

Singer, Isidore, et al. *The Jewish Encyclopedia.* 12 vols. New York: Funk & Wagnalls, 1901–06.

Stillman, Norman A., et al., eds. *Encyclopedia of Jews in the Islamic World.* 5 vols. Boston: Brill, 2010.

Veinstein, Gilles, ed. *Salonique 1850–1918: La "ville des juifs" et le reveil des Balkans.* Paris: Autrement, 1993. Scholarly essays about Salonika in the period from the 1850s through World War I.

Yad Vashem Central Database of Shoah Victims' Names. Accessed June 16, 2015. http://db.yadvashem.org/names/search.html?language=en. Database of Jews persecuted or killed in the Holocaust. Maintained by the Yad Vashem Authority in Israel.

Image sources

All illustrations were scanned from a first-edition copy of *Los israelitas españoles y el idioma castellano*, except as follows:

The portrait of Pinhas Asayag was damaged in the translator's copy of the book. The image used here is from a scan of the page by the Alliance Israélite Universelle, downloaded from the Rachelnet.net database.

There was no author photo in the original book. The portrait used here comes from the Spanish Medicine image bank of Spain's Royal National Academy of Medicine (Real Academia Nacional de la Medicina). Accessed July 18, 2015. http://www.bancodeimagenesmedicina.es.

Illustrations in the *Monde Illustré* article were digitized directly from the 1903 magazine, which the translator located at the New York Public Library. This English edition follows Pulido's book in omitting many of the article's illustrations, but does reinstate one photo missing from the original book (the picture of the modern school) because the text mentions it specifically. A full translation of the French article, with all the magazine illustrations, can be found on the translator's Between Wanderings blog.

The covers of *La Ilustración Española y Americana* and of the *Refranes ó proverbios* book are from Google Books, and did not appear in Pulido's volume.

This edition includes several photos from Pulido's 1905 follow-up book, *Españoles sin patria y la raza sefardí*. Most are portraits of people mentioned in this first book: Lazar

Ascher as an older man, Thamara (Tamara) Ascher, Moïse Fresco's children, and Moritz Levy. The photo of M. Gani also appeared in that sequel volume, but in very poor quality. The image used here is a clearer copy that has circulated online for years. The photo of El Tránsito synagogue, too, appeared in Pulido's second book on Sephardim rather than in this first book.

Obvious dust, dirt, and ink smears have been touched out digitally on some photographs, but with great restraint.

Translator's acknowledgments

Librarians and archivists are the heroes of almost any research project, and I warmly thank the smart, helpful professionals at the New York Public Library's Dorot Jewish Division; the staff of the periodicals department at the Enoch Pratt Free Library in Baltimore; and the Harvard College Library.

This English edition benefitted from the knowledge and wisdom of friends who agreed to read parts of the text and give feedback: Allan Altman (who read and commented on the whole volume), Luis Guzmán Valerio, Warren Hoffman, John McWhorter and J.R. Wilheim. A longtime friend, Dennis Mellor, made one of the research trips a lot more entertaining by turning it into a road trip in his part of the country. Once the translation was done, Toni Kamins was kind enough to help devise some of the promotional material.

Fellow translators in online professional forums gave many thoughtful, well-reasoned answers to arcane queries that I posted. Special thanks go to Danielle Maxson, Edgar Moros, David Pinheiro and Antonio Vizcarra.

I especially thank Mitch Bloom for his patience and supportiveness while I worked on this time-consuming project.

Index

Page numbers in italics mean the subject is mentioned only in a note. This index uses place names from 1904. For modern equivalents, see "A key to 1904 place names" on page xxi.

Ángel Pulido Fernández (1852–1932), Spain's "Apostle of the Sephardic Jews," was an eminent physician, senator, forensic anthropologist, journalist and author. He championed causes ranging from human rights to public health, from social justice to religious tolerance, and from child safety to services for the blind. Besides cofounding the Madrid Press Association, he was, at various times, head of the Madrid School of Midwifery, secretary of Madrid's Anthropology Museum, chairman of the Madrid Board of Physicians, president of the Spanish Child Protection Council, and director of Spain's Department of Health.

From the 1900s to 1920s, this Christian member of Parliament successfully campaigned for Spain to reestablish ties with its exiled Jewish offspring: the Sephardic Jews, whose ancestors the country had banished four centuries earlier. He lectured extensively on the topic and helped to create organizations to promote friendship with Sephardim and make it easier for Jews to immigrate to Spain. In addition to this book (first published in 1904), his Sephardic-themed volumes include *Españoles sin patria y la raza sefardí* (Spaniards without a country and the Sephardic race, 1905) and *Mica: homenaje a la mujer hebrea* (Mica: An homage to Jewish women, 1923).

Steven Capsuto (b. 1964) translates the Between Wanderings book series and edits the Between Wanderings blog, which focus on Jewish social history and culture from the 1850s to 1920s. He grew up in the Philadelphia area in a part-Sephardic, part-Ashkenazic family, and now lives in New York City.

Steven studied translation at Rutgers University and has been a full-time translator since 2003, working from Spanish, French, Catalan, Portuguese and Ladino into English. Professionally, he has translated stage plays, economic forecasts, biomedical texts, family records, websites, corporate newsletters, technical manuals and many other documents. He holds certifications in three language pairs from the American Translators Association.

He is also a nonfiction author: Steven's media-history book *Alternate Channels* was a semifinalist for an American Library Association book award in 2001.

For more information about these books and about Jewish culture and history, visit the

Between Wanderings blog

betweenwanderings.com

44943481R00189

Made in the USA
Middletown, DE
20 June 2017